Airborne

TALES FROM A THOUSAND AND ONE FLIGHTS

To our dear friends -
Andreas & Anna,
thank you for
lovely hospitality 26.2.2013
För Andreas,
Hjärtliga gratuleringar
för 70 års dagen!
Sirpa, Anne

ATAR

Atar Kustannus Oy
www.atar.fi

Airborne:
Tales from a Thousand and One Flights
www.airbornethebook.com

Finnish original:
Taivas mikä työpaikka!

Cover: Juhana Mikkanen
Design: Juhana Mikkanen

Photos: Finnair imagebank and cabin crew member´s personal photo albums
Photos on pages 2-3, 7, 10-14 by Juhana Mikkanen
Riitta Kiiveri´s photo by Sampsa Pärnänen

ISBN 978-952-67577-5-9
Printed in Estonia by Tallinna Raamatutrükikoda OÜ, Tallinn 2012

The photos in the book are not directly related to the stories.

CONTENTS

A NOTE
TO THE READER

Our flight attendants are professionals in customer service, and their creativity, energy and shared will to succeed is often needed at work. We meet millions of passengers per year, and these encounters are a source of countless stories.

The same team spirit, enthusiasm and ability to plunge in head first were expressed by our crew in this book project. This work offers a unique glimpse behind the scenes and into a fascinating world that in spite of some of the glamour of flying having been lost is still full of emotions, situations and interesting people.

This book was written by customer service professionals. I am very proud of the fact that in addition to the actual writing, our team also has nearly all the competence required in publishing a work. Thank you, all of you, who have played a part in creating this book. Welcome, dear readers, aboard this Finnair journey. Sit back, relax, and let our wonderful cabin crew entertain you.

Riitta Vuorelma
Vice President
Inflight Customer Service
Finnair Oyj

PROLOGUE

WITH FINNAIR'S 90TH birthday just around the corner, we, the cabin crew, wanted to put together a book consisting of our own stories, jokes and poems. The sequence of stories began spontaneously with one of our flight attendants sharing her experiences of jetlag on Facebook, followed by numerous similar accounts. One of us then suggested that the stories would be filed or permanently recorded somehow, and practically minutes after the decision to do so was made, the book committee was in existence.

We asked colleagues to share any stories they had, and gradually this book began to take shape. Within two months, we had collected over 600 stories. Retired flight attendants joined in the reminiscing of flying with Aero, and later Finnair, from as early on as the 1950s. One of the ex-flight attendants we interviewed had begun her career in 1953. We received treasured photographs, newspaper clippings, and certificates of honor. The grapevine extended outside of Facebook, with several current and retired flight attendants contacting us and offering their stories. We gladly accepted all the help that was offered.

Finnair was involved early on in the project. The positive attitude of Senior Vice President of Communications and Sustainable Development Arja Suominen and the Vice President of Inflight Customer Service Riitta Vuorelma warmed our hearts. Communications Specialist Laura Varja was also a great help. Brand Manager Taru Kettunen and Vice President of Global Marketing Communications and Brand Management Jarkko Konttinen were delightfully open-minded regarding this project.

We found a publisher and a layout designer easily. Once the background support had been secured, it was easy to proceed. We have tried to capture and maintain the voice of the narrator in every story. The stories are like encounters on flights – brief and intensive. Many of the people photographed on these pages are still actively flying, but we have included also those, whose wings have already been stored among fond memories.

The book committee

FOREWORD

THE ARABIAN NIGHTS: *Tales from a Thousand and One Nights* is familiar to many of us. We have read the book to our children, and perhaps remember ourselves sitting on the laps of our parents or grandparents listening to those stories, which seemed exciting, perhaps even a bit daunting, at the time.

The need to tell stories in the form of fairytales, poems, songs or anecdotes is a fundamental part of being human. The journey from quills to tweets has been long, but it has not changed our will to continue the ancient tradition of narration.

There are innumerable stories about flying, and as it has become an increasingly popular mode of transportation, reaching further and further into all corners of the world, these stories have become increasingly vivid.

We often fly to destinations that have been shaken up by one disaster or another. In those situations, there always seems to be a member of the crew who can break the tension with a good story. When exhaustion is taking its toll, or we are weighed down by uncertainty, joy and laughter give us energy. The ability to live in the moment, to give it all that we've got, and to rely on situational comedy, are our sources of strength.

To all of us, who have felt wind beneath our wings, the experience has been remarkable. On our work trips, we can tap into an alternative reality that differs from the everyday routine.

To the reader, we would like to wish a pleasant journey with us to the far edge of the world and back.

Fly, fly high
in the soft lap of the fair-weather cloud.
As the sun casts its golden fan on the sea
You are free.

Riitta Kiiveri

THE BOOK
COMMITTEE

RIITTA KIIVERI

The United States has always played a big part in Riitta's life. After a year as an exchange student in Illinois, Riitta worked as a flight attendant for Pan American World Airways, based in Boston. She returned to Finland to study, and after completing a degree in tourism, she started working for Finnair as a flight attendant, and later became a Finn Hostess on long-haul routes. After 10 years of flying, she found herself in the USA again, this time in California's Long Beach. Her employment with Finnair continued while there, and later in Germany as well. After returning to Finland, Riitta worked for several years as Route Catering Manager of Inflight Service at Finnair Catering, and completed a degree in classic homeopathy while working. Riitta returned to flying in 2004. Cooking, golf, homeopathy and writing are some of her dear hobbies.

TONY POKKINEN

There were several things Tony wanted to be when he grew up: a set designer, lighting designer, actor or chef. On his first Finnair flight to Palma de Mallorca as a 12-year-old, Tony dropped all other plans and decided to become an airline steward. Before he started flying for a living, he still managed to put in a few years as a waiter and bartender in quality restaurants and on Silja Line's cruise ships. Tony joined Finnair in 1988. He later worked as a Service Chef, a flight attendant specialized in business class service. He has also worked as a service trainer. On the side, Tony owns a travel and event business, arranging, for example, Caribbean cruises for cabin crew. He was pressured by his friends to participate in Master Chef Finland in 2011, and made it to the final 14. These days, he loves cooking at home with his partner.

NOORA KUNTTU

Already as a little girl, Noora would line up some chairs, ask her parents and au pair to sit on them, and serve her passengers food and drinks. Her father, who traveled a lot, once hit the souvenir jackpot by bringing her a child-size British Airways flight attendant's apron. Flying was always her dream job, but unfortunately, she was a little too short. She had to let go of her dream, and began studying Finnish at university. As fate would have it, one day, Finnair lowered the height requirement for a cabin crew, and Noora could finally apply. She was accepted, and felt like she had come home. She has been flying for nine years now. At Finnair, she has also worked as a safety instructor, and written her own blog about flying. In summer, she spends most of her free time sailing with her husband and her dog, and in winter, she writes interior design articles and attends pilates classes.

PIRKKO SAARI

After graduating from high school, Pirkko went to Switzerland to study French language and literature, and to figure out what she wanted to be when she grew up. After two years, she met her future husband and returned to Finland. She started flying at Finnair in 1988, but never thought she would end up staying for very long. She was recently amazed to realize that she has had wings on her jacket for more than half her life now. As a talkative extrovert, she enjoys her work, even though its tempo has changed from waltz to samba. For several years, Pirkko used to be an on-the-job trainer, helping new flight attendants on their first flights. She has studied while working, and has completed a commercial degree and various courses. The rest of her time awake goes into strengthening the wings of her teenage children.

CHRISTINA STRANDBERG

Chisu decided early on what she would be when she grew up. However, there were three choices: a writer, a physical education instructor, or a flight attendant. She spent a year in the United States as an exchange student. After returning to Finland and graduating from high school, Chisu applied to Finnair, but was still too young. She got a secretarial degree while waiting for the time to pass. She began flying in 1988. Exercise and literature have remained important hobbies and stress-relievers over the years. Working as a flight attendant has changed significantly in 24 years, but the wonderful team spirit among colleagues keeps her motivated and happy at work. Her "crazy" colleagues have recently talked her into all kinds of projects. Her motto is: if you can dream it, you can do it! You get what you ask for!

MERIITTA AHTIKARI

When three-year-old Meriitta stepped into Aero's (Finnair), DC-3 with her mother and older brothers, she knew immediately what she would become when she grew up. The flight attendant clad in a stylish uniform made an unforgettable impression on her, as she placed Meriitta's meal tray on a white tablecloth in front of her. The atmosphere on the flight was so dignified that little Meriitta decided to eat just like the other passengers – with a knife and fork! Her childhood dream came true when she was chosen for Finnair's cabin crew training course in 1975. On the blue-and-white wings, she has worked as a specially trained Finn Hostess on long-haul routes, and later as a purser. In addition, she has graduated from the University of Helsinki as a speech therapist, and is also a qualified consultant in wellbeing at work. She has two children who have already flown the nest.

KATI KAIVANTO

As a young high school graduate in her hometown Tampere, Kati dreamt of becoming a physical education teacher. She attended Varala Sports Institute and worked as a substitute P.E. teacher for a year, until she saw an advertisement in the newspaper for Finnair's cabin crew training course and decided to give it a try. One day, her acceptance letter came in the mail. She is still on that same road she took in 1978. On the way, she became the mother of three daughters, who were born a year apart, and stayed at home with them for six years. In addition to working as a flight attendant, she has modeled, and even had a small role in the TV series *Love Boat*. Drawing, painting and writing remain close to Kati's heart.

LENE MALMSTRÖM

Lene joined Finnair right after graduation. She wanted to try flying, and this trial has now lasted 25 years. Our energetic flight attendant works in "the beach ball group", meaning that she mainly works on leisure flights operated by the Boeing 757.

Since the youngest of Lene's children is not yet at school, she works part time, and flying is a nice change from household chores. Her oldest children have already moved out. Exercising is one of Lene's passions, and she likes trying new forms of exercise on her work trips, for example, hot yoga in Halifax, Canada, and hiking in Osaka, Japan. Lene loves animals, especially dogs.

CHAPTER 1

WHO WE ARE

MANY CHARACTERISTICS ARE expected from flight attendants: we have to have emotional intelligence and enjoy being with people, but at the same time, we need to be able to be cool and authoritative in an emergency. Flight attendants are energetic and adapt quickly to different situations. A flight attendant is probably the first person to start distributing life-vests when the engine of a speed boat fails on holiday in Thailand. A flight attendant will break up a bar brawl, resuscitate a drunk on the street, and tell the person dialing emergency services what to say. Organizing is in our blood, and a flight attendant will always know what to do or say.

Flight attendants usually do not know the rest of the crew beforehand. To start the day, we introduce ourselves, and then dive right into the data regarding our flight. On the way to the aircraft we are already talking about other things. The trip from the Crew Center to the rear galley is filled with stories of our divorces, illnesses of our family members, troubles of our teenagers, happy moments, work history before Finnair, studies, summer cottages and boats. We might not remember each other's names, but we will probably remember each other's life stories. We share secrets and offer advice and support. When the aircraft is airborne, we are already old friends. Some of us may have spent more Christmases with colleagues than with our own families. This creates a unique work atmosphere, and indeed, most of us say that wonderful colleagues are the reason we enjoy our work so much.

"WHAT DO WE DO AND BUY HERE?"

Flight attendants lead irregular lives. A nine-to-five job would be horrifying to most of us, who occasionally have trouble knowing what day of the week it is; there are only work days and days off. Routines are created by different means; we are creatures of habit on layovers, often doing the same things at the same destinations, dining and shopping in the same places, time and time again. We tend to be gregarious; if one of us finds a good massage parlor or buys something with very good value for money, hundreds of colleagues will soon follow. On arrival at a new destination, we ask our colleagues, "What do we do and buy here?"

Our children get their fair share of flying. Occasionally we are able to take them along on our work trips, and often bring exciting presents for them. Children learn at an early age how to escape from a burning building, or climb on to a life raft (or rubber dinghy at the summer cottage). They are polite and friendly, and always introduce themselves to the crew on board. On a typical morning, a pre-flight briefing will end with a couple of flight attendants calling home to make sure their children are awake for school.

BEEN AROUND THE BLOCK A FEW TIMES

You will seldom see a disconcerted flight attendant; we have been around the block – more than a few times. When a work trip can be extended by a week due to a volcanic ash cloud, or you are short of 37 passenger meals on a flight, you are not easily thrown out of sync, and learn to come up with solutions quickly. Colleagues will help each other in anything and everything. When the volcanic ash cloud hovering above Europe left several flight attendants stranded around the world, colleagues here in Finland made sure that their children had babysitters, and organized car-pools to schools and hobbies. When Japan suffered a massive earthquake followed by a deadly tsunami, we immediately began collecting supplies, and every flight attendant flying to Japan carried diapers, blankets, clothes, baby formula and any other items that were desperately needed, with them. There were more than enough volunteers for evacuation flights from Thailand that followed the tsunami in 2004.

Since our rosters are published only for a month at a time, and seven days prior to the end of the previous month, life cannot be planned ahead in very much detail. Indeed, flight attendants are masters of living in the moment. We miss many birthdays and anniversaries, and can seldom participate in all the events we would want to. We make up for it any way we can. Mothers of young children enjoy uninterrupted sleep and a little time to themselves (not to mention beautifully laid out hotel breakfasts!) on layovers, even if they miss their little ones at the same time. Crew that have to spend Christmas away celebrate together, and if any champagne is left over from the Business Class service, we cannot bear pouring the noble drink down the drain, but baptize recent recruits by washing their hands with it instead.

HURRY, HURRY!

Some things are in our blood. Even if we are pulled out of bed in the middle of the night, we will remember our training. This literally happened to one of our flight attendants, when her husband, a pilot, had a nightmare that there was something wrong with the aircraft he was flying. He decided that evacuation was necessary, and began shouting, "Hurry, hurry! This way!" in his sleep. A flight attendant won't question orders given to her in an emergency, so she immediately leaped out of bed and rushed into the hallway. The husband followed. Only at the door did they finally wake up – luckily, considering it was winter and the couple was in their night attire.

ODE TO BLUE-AND-WHITE STEWARDESSES

What are little stewardesses made of?
Hazy dreams,
the flight of fairies,
songs of strange winds
calling from afar
to see and experience it all.

What are stewardesses' dreams made of?
Champagne and kisses,
Sleeping Beauty's fantasies,
Cinderella's hopes and dreams,
handsome princes of fancy castles,
fairyshoes of silk,
ballrooms and endless dances.

What are older stewardesses made of?
The sumptuous scent of fire roses,
shimmering pearls,
quiet waves of the wide ocean,
the majestic flight of white swans,
vintages of memories of flights gone by.

Sirpa Kivilaakso

CREW STORIES

I'M A FAIRLY junior flight attendant with young children, and I fearfully awaited December roster publication, as I was hoping to spend Christmas at home. When I finally saw my roster I burst into tears. According to the roster, I would be on standby duty for five days over Christmas, meaning that I could be called out to any Finnair long-haul destination on short notice. An image of me in a lonely hotel room in Phuket, clutching a photo of my children tightly in my hand, flashed through my mind. I put my standby duty on offer in the flight exchange pool, but did not have very high hopes for a swap. However, on the following morning, a male colleague called, saying he would gladly swap my standby for his short-haul flights, and offered to swap the whole beginning of the month, if that would help in getting the swap accepted. I immediately accepted the offer, as I would now at least be

home in the evenings over the holidays. My little five-year-old cried for joy, but so did I, when I thought about the kindness and generosity of my colleague. The childless steward had understood how important it was for me to be able to spend Christmas with my children. It was the best Christmas present of my life.

AN ACQUAINTANCE OF mine often asked me to bring all kinds of things from my work trips: toilet radios that played music, silk, shoes, clothes, golf equipment and what not. Gradually, I got annoyed, and finally wrote a shopping list for my acquaintance: milk, cheese, eggs, coffee, orange juice, bread. The acquaintance appeared bewildered and asked, "What's this? Am I to do your grocery shopping?" I calmly replied, "Why not, I run after your shopping all over the world, don't I?" In this case, it was not the beginning of a beautiful friendship.

"WHAT ARE YOU, A COP?"

ONCE UPON A time at a taxi stand in Helsinki… The bars had just closed, so the queue for taxis was very long. There was some argument in the queue about whose turn it was, and soon a fist fight broke out. Two men fell over, and one started kicking the other in the head. Without any hesitation, I jumped in and took down the attacker, who was larger than me, but luckily too surprised to retaliate. People standing in line began to clap, and someone asked, "What are you, a cop?" "No, I'm a flight attendant," I replied with a bright smile, and was then offered a place at the head of the queue…

THE HUSBAND OF a flight attendant was concerned that his wife shared their personal affairs a little too freely at work. He said he would soon have to fly with other airlines, as he feared his wife's colleagues might laugh at him. He shouldn't have worried; flight attendants don't laugh at each other's problems. We know that each one of us goes through rough patches every now and then.

CHAPTER 2

FIRST STEPS

IN 2012, THE Finnish flight attendant will be 65 years old, as the first flight that had a flight attendant onboard took place on 21 June, 1947. The aircraft was a DC-3, operating a domestic flight from Helsinki to Kemi. The first male cabin stewards in Finland started working at the end of the 1950s, but Daimler Airways had hired stewards as early as in 1922. They were called *cabin boys*, and their duties were to assist passengers and convince them that flying was safe. In 1930, Boeing Air transport hired the first female flight attendants, now known as *the original eight*. Steven Stimpson, who was employed by the airline, had an idea that it would be useful to have flight attendants onboard. He had been on a flight that had been badly delayed, and there was nobody to look after the passengers. Civil aviation was dominated by men, and in addition to Steve, it took one brave woman, a nurse called Ellen Church, to convince the airline board that women could and should be hired. In addition to Ellen, seven other female flight attendants were hired, and they are the true pioneers of the profession.

In those days, flight attendants' duties were quite different from what they are today. Or what would you say about flight attendants picking up passengers from their homes on the way to the airport, and then making another stop to buy the meals that were served onboard? At the airport, they would weigh passengers' luggage and the mail that was carried, after first helping the passengers onboard. Flight attendants were advised to rinse their mouths with mouthwash before starting the meal service, to ensure an all-round fresh image. Delivering mail was the top priority in those days; if the aircraft was too heavy, the flight attendant would be offloaded first, and after her the passengers, but the mail would always be delivered to its destination.

As flying increased in popularity, celebrities took off too. Flight attendant training at Pan American Airways included a special "Gable Routine", in which the company's first stewards were taught how a celebrity such as Clark Gable should be treated while his luggage was getting weighed.

In post-war Finland, there were material shortages, and many young people wanted to experience something new and healing. They felt that their youth would go to waste if spent in an atmosphere that was stagnant and spiritually stifling. Aviation was an attractive option for young women who craved excitement, and perhaps a good husband.

GRADUATING FORM THE CHAMBER OF HORRORS WITH HONORS

Aero's (known as Finnair today) first flight attendants were Eija Louhi, Clara Majblom, Kaarina Wendelin, Inger Möller, Eija Merisalo and Gigi Hohenthal. Before they were hired, they had to endure language tests, spinning chairs, the decompression chamber, monochromatic tests, giving injections to people, and other psychophysical tests, which at the time, were much the same as what pilots had to undergo. These young

women had dreamt of flying, and finally in 1947, they were given wings.

In an issue of the Finnish magazine Seura from 1964, Kari Tuomi describes the entrance examination that Arja Tuomarila, known also as a singer and TV announcer, participated in. The first part of the exam was the decompression chamber test, which was also known as the chamber of horrors. The purpose was to test the participant's physical ability to equalize pressure, particularly in organs that contain air, such as the ears and sinuses. Arja went up to the altitude of five kilometers without any problems. The doctor monitoring the exam was satisfied and lit a cigarette.

The next phase was a stress test. A flight attendant's job requires good physical health, and the stress test evaluated the heart's ability to pump blood effectively to different parts of the body. Arja felt her heart beat very fast, and thought she had cycled at least a dozen kilometers, even though the actual distance was only a few. A blood test was taken immediately after the decompression chamber and stress tests. If the test would have shown any irregularity in blood circulation at an altitude, the applicant would have been sent home. After the blood test, Arja's back and leg extensor muscles were tested. The final part of the physical examination was the spinning chair, which was spun at a great speed and then suddenly stopped, in order to check if the applicant would get sea-sick, and be able to distinguish how many fingers the examiner held up. Arja passed, and her physical examination was soon followed by psychological aptitude and language tests.

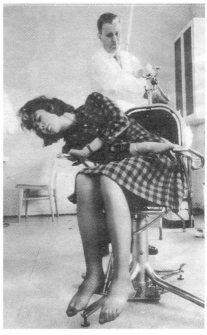

Finnair did well in picking Arja for the job; she continued flying until 2008. Today she is an active pensioner, who still sings with her husband, Kai Lind (an actor and musician).

THE NAME OF THE GAME IS TRUST

In the old days, some young women only wanted to try flying for a couple of years, but many ended up staying for decades. Miss Finland of 1961, Ritva Wächter, worked as a flight attendant for 46 years, which is a record in Finland. During her career, she worked on 13 different aircraft types.

The navy blue uniform, golden buttons decorated with Finland's lion coat of arms, a bright white blouse, and the hat made a flight attendant feel like a queen. In 1952, the year the Olympic Games were held in Finland, the Seutula Airport was opened, and Aero acquired some new Convair-440 aircraft. The post-war atmosphere was more hopeful now, and travelling abroad became easier.

A flight attendant who began her career in 1953, explained how the crew used to buy Bata shoes in Amsterdam, as nothing like them were available in Finland at the time. Trendy jersey clothes and suits were bought in a tiny store in Stockholm called H&M... Flight attendants went to the opera in Amsterdam, and learned how to eat fondue in Basel.

In the old days, there weren't that many flight attendants at Aero. They were like a close-knit family, and everyone knew each other's joys and sorrows. On domestic layovers, the crew stayed at a house called Bird's Nest, which the company had rented. Everyone brought their own bed linen with them, and at the end of a work day, the flight attendants would cook for the pilots and themselves. Shopping for groceries was the first officer's responsibility. It was natural for romances to blossom and wither in that environment – the crew spent so much time together. A strong sense of community and togetherness has always been typical for the profession; colleagues have always looked out for each other, and now, in the era of Facebook and other means of social media, this sense of community has only become stronger. In the past, after a long flight, the crew would gather in someone's hotel room for a debriefing,

THE IRISES OF AMSTERDAM

In the haze of a November evening
a long, long time ago
Vincent sprinkled
a stubble field
spiraling stars
- and irises
on canvas.

Nobody understood.

Only much, much later
did the irises fly
to the country of cherry blossoms
to become stars.

Sirpa Kivilaakso

to have a drink and discuss any unpleasant or funny occurrences on the flight. This helped the crew to cope with any work-related problems. In the era of shorter layovers, debriefings tend to take place in Facebook groups; "writing it out of one's system" has become a new way of dealing with work pressure.

However, inflight therapy has not disappeared. We have time to listen to each other's troubles on long night flights; we ask and give advice freely. These discussions are strictly confidential, and cabin crew gossip surprisingly little about each other. We all understand the nature of the job; we are together for one trip, and the next time we meet might be years from now, so there is no time for sowing circles or cliques to form. We have the best colleagues in the world!

CHAPTER 3

IN THE OLD DAYS

TRAVELLING AND FLYING from one place to another have always been the upside of the job. As a flight attendant, the world would be accessible to you in stages: new recruits would first start on domestic routes, then move on to Europe, and eventually North America. On leisure flights, the whole world was your oyster. Kar-Air, previously Karhumäki Airways, was a charter company founded by brothers Karhumäki. Kar-Air operated Finnair's leisure traffic until the companies merged in the early 1990s. In spite of the merger, crew with B-757 qualifications flying mainly leisure flights continue to be called "the beach ball group". Leisure flights carry passengers to destinations that are not accessible on scheduled flights. As these destinations are often far away, the crew get to stay at holiday destinations, often for days – hence the name. In the past, flight schedules were more infrequent, and even crew working on scheduled flights got to enjoy long layovers. For many, this was the golden era of flying; there was time for one's body clock to adjust, and even time for sightseeing. Today, most of our layovers barely last 24 hours.

In the 1950s, Finns didn't speak foreign languages as fluently as today, and any language skills acquired abroad were a benefit for would-be flight attendants. Flying as a profession broadened the social circle of many young women and men. Air travel used to be a luxury that only a few could afford; however, as ticket prices decreased, flying became accessible to people from all walks of life. Flight attendants, particularly those working in first class, learned to discuss all kinds of issues with passen-

THE RED SKY OF SUNSET

The dark, quiet sea
gently rocked the boats to sleep.
The caress of the winds
slowly drew in the night.
Even the seagulls were silent.

Kati Kaivanto

gers. There was more time for socializing with passengers than there is today, and indeed, interaction with different kinds of people was a big part of working as a flight attendant. The ability to get along with people, and enjoying their company were important criteria for the job. In addition, flight attendants had to be attractive: a pleasing sight for men's eyes. Young and handsome cabin stewards naturally appealed to female customers.

CONVERSATIONAL SKILLS
AND TIME FOR THE CUSTOMERS

Service-mindedness was a prerequisite for applicants, as nearly everything else could be taught. The detailed training of flight attendants included food and beverage knowledge, table settings, serving cheese and wine... Very few families in Finland served either cheese or wine at home in the 1950s and 1960s.

Anja-Brita Huttunen, Head Stewardess at the time, had a clear idea on what direction cabin service should take already in 1969, when Finnair's scheduled flights to North America began. She created the concept of the Finn Hostess, who had time for passengers in need of

extra assistance, for example, families travelling with children. In many ways, Finn Hostesses were Finnair's business card in the sky. These flight attendants were educated in Finnish history, art, architecture, and tourist attractions. One could say that Finnair's "Peace of Mind" concept began back then. Passengers flying over the Atlantic enjoyed the unhurried service of the Finn Hostesses, and delicious À la Carte meals served on crockery designed by Tapio Wirkkala. Beverages

were served in Ulthima Thule glasses, which were especially designed for Finnair and still in use today. The table clothes were Dora Jung linen, and sleepy passengers were covered with Marjatta Metsovaara's designer blankets. In addition to a special uniform, the Finn Hostess wore a silver brooch designed by Björn Weckström, the first item in his Space Design series. The pin depicted a space age human looking for another of his kind in a strange environment. Björn Weckström's space jewelry was later worn by Princess Leia in the Star Wars films. Modern Finnair pays homage to its design heritage: the current uniforms are designed by Ritva-Liisa Pohjalainen, echoing the traditions of the past but looking towards the future, with a new, peaceful interior design for the aircraft cabin to match.

Finn Hostesses were later replaced by Service Chefs, giving an opportunity for men to specialize in business class service as well.

In addition to helping in designing new service concepts, the head stewardess had an important role in the company. She was the flight attendants' supervisor, and stood up for her subordinates in work-related matters. She participated in planning their training, and occasionally taught herself. Nowadays, the Finnish Cabin Crew Union safeguards flight attendants' work conditions. The first flight attendants, for example, Aero's first Head Stewardess Clara Majblom, were often trained nurses, and taught first aid and patient care to their colleagues.

As the years went by, flight attendants developed their skills in reading situations, and soon knew how to act around an unaccompanied minor, the president, a king, a captain of industry, or a nervous flyer.

HANDBRAKE

Handbrake on,
can barely move.
I have flown
to Hong Kong and back
in 48 hours.

Riitta Kiiveri

Flight attendants were able to shop abroad for clothes, cosmetics, home textiles, glassware and crockery. Some even bought luxury materials that were not available in Finland for the house they were building.

The downside of flying was that it wasn't really considered a proper profession. It was a dream job in many ways, but still had a bad reputation. Most people only flew for a few years; there was little chance of any advancement, and women with university degrees did not want to see themselves ageing on the aircraft aisle. Practically the only way up within the company was to become an assistant of the inspector stewardess. The title of Purser was not introduced until the 1970s, when flying finally became a job you could retire from.

Irregular working hours often created havoc in the lives of young married couples, with the wife and/or

mother away a lot. When she was at home, she was always tired. Even unmarried young women struggled, as their work and leisure time often overlapped. At worst, flight attendants found themselves trapped in a vicious cycle of stress and sleeping disorders. However, few dared to quit, even if it would have been good for them and their families – women were concerned about their ability to adjust to normal life after several years of such a different lifestyle. Those that stayed found life easier as the years went by, and their ability to prioritize and put things into proportion improved. Having worked as a flight attendant continues to be a source of pride and joy for many who have retired years ago. Looking after other people, be they customers or colleagues has become second nature. Finnair, or the "blue-and-white wings", have always been a source of pride for flight crew, and the team spirit among employees is clearly one of the company's strengths.

CREW STORIES

IN MOSCOW BACK in the 1950s, our hotel was very close to the airport. The rooms didn't have proper doors that locked, and since we were personally responsible for the money from inflight sales, the chief of cabin would sleep with the money under her pillow.

ON FLIGHTS TO Oulu, there used to be a four hours' wait before the return flight. If the weather was warm, we'd sunbathe by the tarmac, wearing only lingerie. We'd take our nylons off; they were quite expensive at the time, so we looked after them as well as we could in all situations. Our uniforms were navy blue, and they had golden buttons bearing the Finnish national lion emblem. We used to fly a lot of mail delivery flights with the DC-3. There was no place to sit on those cargo flights, so we'd sit on these huge sacks of mail. On flights from Helsinki to Kuopio we used to carry mail, and passengers only on the way back. In Kuopio, we had time to go for a swim at a nearby lake, and would come back refreshed for the return flight.

FROM THE 1950S to the 1970s, uniform regulations were very strict. Jewelry was forbidden; makeup had to be light, and longer than collar-length hair had to be tied back. If you put on too much weight, you would be grounded for a month, and had to lose those extra pounds within that time. Another form of punishment was to put the flight attendant on domestic service for a month. Even the passengers knew about this form of punishment, and would ask stewardesses on domestic flights, "What did you do?" If you were sick on a national holiday, the company nurse might show up on your doorstep to check if you actually were ill!

THE INSPECTOR STEWARDESS once said to a stunningly beautiful flight attendant, "You really should pay attention to your weight and alcohol consumption!" The voluptuous flight attendant looked at the inspector in the eyes and replied, "You pay attention to yourself first – you look like a flower pot flipped upside down!" She walked away calmly and left the inspector stewardess to huff and puff all by herself.

AT THE END of the 1960s, domestic flights used to be operated with the DC-3, which didn't have a PA system. Instead of making an announcement, the first officer would fill in a little note with the flight details, which included the weather at the destination, the arrival time and the last names of the crew. One day, the passengers were convinced that the crew was having fun at their expense. The crew list read: Captain Kotka (Eagle), First Officer Pyy (Grouse), Stewardess Leivonen (Skylark) and Trainee Stewardess Sorsa (Duck). It was a genuine coincidence!

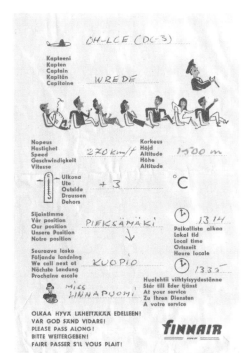

THE AIRCRAFT DOOR was sometimes slightly ajar, as the aircraft flew very low, and the cabin was not pressurized. Just imagine the noise! There was a coat-hanger above every passenger seat for the passengers' coats. We would put the coats on the hangers and hang them up on a clothes rail at the back of the cabin before takeoff. This required some strength, especially with heavy winter coats and a full flight. Flights were rather short, so almost immediately after takeoff, we'd have to take those coats back to the passengers for landing.

WE WERE ON our way to Bardufoss in Northern Norway, when the pilots told me that they had forgotten to take a map along, and asked, if I had one. "Yes, it so happens I do," I replied, "But just a small pocket-sized one in my calendar, so I doubt such a place is even marked on it…" "Don't worry," said the captain, "It's close to Tromssa,

so if we can just find our way there first, we can then ask the air traffic control for directions." Don't worry indeed! I guess my little pocket calendar and its map saved that flight.

FLIGHT ATTENDANTS COULD double as weather girls in the 1960s. "It was raining heavily in Stockholm when we left," I said to my farmer neighbor after I got home. He was very grateful for this piece of information, and headed straight out to the field. Usually the same weather would reach Finland approximately a day later.

"MISS, FOR THE LOVE OF GOD, WOULD YOU MAKE UP YOUR MIND ALREADY!"

THIS HAPPENED ON a domestic flight in Northern Finland. We would do several short flights a day, and sometimes it got hard to keep track of where we were headed. On an early morning, I welcomed the passengers onboard and announced our destination, which caused some restlessness in the cabin. I realized I had announced the wrong place and tried again, but the anxiety only increased. We were already taxiing so I had no place to check. A passenger turned to me in exasperation and said, "Miss, for the love of God, would you make up your mind already!" I replied in panic, "Please tell me where we are, so I'll remember where we're headed!"

IN WINTER TIME, portable heaters were brought in to warm the cabin on the DC-3. Sometimes the cold was so bad that we'd put the hot air blowers under our skirts to keep warm...

THE DC-3 HAD landed in Rovaniemi, and the pilots asked me to come into the cockpit while we were still taxiing. I opened the door, and the entire cabin could see how a white reindeer was trotting in front of the aircraft. The pilots slowed down, so that the reindeer could safely get off the runway and into the nearby forest.

IN THE 1960S, I accidentally announced, "Ladies and gentlemen, Captain Laaksonen and his band would like to welcome you all onboard..." Well, in a way, we're all performing artists.

CARRYING SINGERS AND HUSQVARNAS

FINNAIR PILOTS WERE issued uniform bags that they claimed looked like old sewing machines, so they were known to all flight crew as Singers. It was only natural then that SAS pilots carried Husqvarnas. For a long time, there was a persistent belief that in case of a crash, the rear part of the aircraft was the safest place to be in. On the Super Caravelle, a flight attendant usually stood in front of the last row during boarding, as we preferred to keep it to ourselves. Two SAS pilots embarked in Stockholm carrying their Husqvarnas, heading for that last row. "The rear part will stay in one piece if there's a crash," the pilots offered. "No, my dear sirs," I replied, "I guarantee that in the event of a crash, the aircraft will break just here," and pointed at the last row. "Very well," they conceded laughing, and sat on the very first row instead.

I REMEMBER A particularly bad day at work, after which I sat in my garden. A nightingale began to sing, and I began to cry. A little hedgehog came out of nowhere and gently pushed its head against my toes. Sometimes nature comes to our consolation, and having a good cry helps.

IN THE 1960S, a passenger said that he had lost his contact lenses onboard. We tried to help him look, but we actually had no idea what we were looking for – contact lenses didn't exist in Finland at the time! We nodded to each other and pretended to look for them, thinking that the passenger was probably off his rocker.

Flight attendants used to go to the bonded warehouse before the flight, and personally check how much alcohol would be loaded on the flight. They were responsible for any discrepancies with bonded items or money.

THE CARAVELLE HAD a portable PA handset. A steward wanted to make a little joke, came into the cabin with the handset, and told the stewardess that her mother was calling to check if she had remembered to wear her woolen panties on such a cold day. The passengers were amused and amazed with this modern technology.

"MUMMY! THAT POLICEWOMAN IS STARING AT ME!"

ON FLIGHTS FROM Copenhagen to Helsinki, we used to serve steak tartar sandwiches, and put a raw egg yolk on them as a finishing touch. In order to keep the eggs safe, we would keep the cartons on our laps during takeoff.

IN THE 1970S, wigs made of kanekalon fiber were very popular. I think I owned three, because they were easy to wear at work; I'd just pull my hair back on a tight bun and put the wig on.

However, the attendant call button on the Caravelle was a death-trap for wigs. Nothing was as embarrassing as a wig dangling from the call button as you reached over to serve drinks to the window seat…

AT THE START of the war between Iran and Iraq, Finnair got the last Finns out with a special evacuation flight. We flew down with a Caravelle, and fighter jets escorted us into Teheran. At the airport, soldiers were guarding the doors. The Finnish Ambassador came into the cockpit and was very nervous. I spiked his coffee with cognac without the guards noticing. "Thank you, I feel so much better now! Now let's get our people home!" he said, and off we went.

A GROUP OF well-built men embarked, on their way to a destination in Europe. On the flight, some of them said that they were worried since they were carrying extra weight. "Oh, don't worry," I said, "You're already onboard and apparently you didn't have to pay extra?" The men looked bewildered. "No, we're carrying the extra weight on our bodies!" They were the Finnish national wrestling team, and some of them still had to drop a few pounds. We had two hours to go, so for the rest of the flight, the empty cargo hold number six (accessible from the cabin) served as a gym. I don't know whether or not the exercise session worked.

THERE WAS USUALLY only one flight attendant working on the Convair Metropolitan. I was standing at the door welcoming passengers in Mariehamn, and smiled at a little girl, who had sat down on the first row with her mother. "Mummy! That policewoman is staring at me!" she said. I suppose our uniform wasn't very appealing to children.

ON MIDSUMMER EVE, there was only one passenger onboard the Convair Metropolitan. The pilots told me to ask the passenger if he had a summer cottage, and where it might be. I did, and since the cottage was on our route, the pilots flew low by it, to the passenger's great surprise and amusement. We took a slight detour past my summer cottage and the pilots' cottages as well. Flights really weren't that hectic at all back in the 1970s.

A PASSENGER WAS bitter after I had rejected his affections. When he showed up on my flight years later, he remarked cattily, "So, are you at the height of your career now?" I said "Yes, of course." We were flying at an altitude of 5,000 meters after all.

"THERE ARE RATS HERE..."

SOME CARDBOARD BOXES were loaded into hold number six from Stockholm to Helsinki, but I hadn't checked to see what was in them. During boarding, I saw a flash of something white next to my jumpseat. I took a closer look, and saw that there were two white rats in the corner next to the hold. I informed the cockpit of my findings, but

the pilots never got back to me, and off we went! Luckily, the rats were well-behaved, and stayed in that corner for the duration of the flight. Once we got to Helsinki, the pilots requested five white cats, since we already had five white-faced stewardesses, and five boxes of white rats onboard!

IN 1978, WE flew to Rovaniemi with the DC-9, and comedian Danny Kaye was onboard with an American film crew. He was very charming to us, of course, and said we looked so young we must have just been born. I have dark hair and brown eyes, so I guess I stood out from the other flight attendants. "How is this possible, everyone in Finland is blonde," he remarked. "Yes, it must be my Lappish blood," I joked back. "No," he said, grabbed the handset from my hand and announced, "This young woman is wearing contact lenses, and no-one in Finland can have such brown eyes!" Oh, those were the days!

A PASSENGER HAD bought some lobsters, intending to serve them to his dinner guests later that evening, and asked me, if I could keep them refrigerated during the flight. I wanted to be helpful, and took them to the rear hold, which on the Caravelle was right behind the actual cabin area. We stopped in Stockholm before our final destination, and the cargo hold was emptied there. The lobsters were offloaded there too since I forgot to take them out in time... I had no idea how to make up for my blunder to the poor dinner host. Fortunately, the man was incredibly understanding, and said he would just pick something up from Hotel Kämp on his way home. Even the lobsters were eventually relocated in Stockholm, but naturally their "best before" date was long gone.

ONE OF THE most memorable flights of my career carried Vietnamese refugees from Amsterdam to Helsinki. I asked Catering to deliver some sweets that we could give to the children after the meal service. I was touched that the children had never seen or tasted sweets before, and I cried as I served them. Many, many years later, I met one of these children again; he was working as a postman, and was delivering the mail to my house. We recognized each other straight away, and hugged and cried for minutes, before I could let him continue with his round.

"PLEASE, JUST DON'T HIT ME AGAIN!"

THE DC-9 WAS full of salesmen on their way back from Paris, and they had all had more than a few drinks. As I was pushing the sales trolley along the aisle, I suddenly felt a hand reaching up under my skirt. I didn't pause to think, but punched the arm of the man sitting on the aisle seat with all my strength. From his surprised expression, I immediately made the conclusion that I had the wrong man! I was still too angry to even apologize for my mistake, and carried on with the sales. Once I had calmed down, I thought it might be a good idea to apologize and explain to the man whom I had wrongfully punished, and went back to his seat. "I'm really sorry about what happened," I said. "But when I was here earlier, something extremely unpleasant happened, and I couldn't ignore it. I'm not sorry that I hit someone, but I am sorry that I hit the wrong man." The passenger suggested that we meet later, so that I could tell him the whole story. "No, I can't do that," I answered, and nudged his arm in a friendly manner (or so I thought), "Can we just agree to part ways in peace, here and now?" The passenger grinned and replied, "Yes, yes, of course... Please, just don't hit me again!"

CHAPTER 4

LEAVING HOME

EVERY FLIGHT IS a new experience, even if you have been doing this job for decades. No flight attendant can just shut the front door and leave, as there are usually dozens of things that need attention. Those of us who have families usually have a long checklist to complete: who is picking up the children from daycare, or looking after them altogether, if my spouse is away on a business trip? Have I cooked enough food and bought enough groceries? Is the laundry done? Who is making sure the children's homework gets done, taking the dog out, and will anyone remember to feed the fish while I'm gone? Single people have similar concerns; cats and dogs need looking after, plants need to be watered and bills paid on time. Layovers are not as long as they used to be, but anything can still happen. Aircraft break down, volcanoes erupt, heavy rains flood roads, snowstorms shut down airports, and thunderstorms circle around, while passengers and crew wait impatiently to get home. Even air traffic controllers might go on strike. You might still feel jet-lagged from the previous trip while already packing for a new one. Long trips are taxing for flight crew, and it is hard to make up for lost sleep.

"SHE IS CRYING AND VACUUMING AT HOME – NAKED"

We sometimes feel sorry for our loved ones, who have to put up with all kinds of things that our irregular schedules cause. We seldom even realize the impact that our job has on our behavior. "How do you recognize a flight attendant who's just come back from New York?" The answer is, of course, "She's crying and vacuuming at home – naked." Hearing this joke, many of us have wondered who's been peeking in from our windows…

There are many stories about the departure rituals of flight crew, and their strangeness is usually in direct proportion to the length of the layover. One will go to the gym for a double workout, since there will be no time to exercise on the layover. Another will clean house from top to bottom and iron all the clothes before leaving – the "clean slate" approach. A third might not be able to accomplish anything before work, except lie on the couch and gather strength, with her family tiptoeing around and saying, "Shhh, she'll be leaving soon..."

One of my colleagues says that she cooks meals in advance and puts labels with dates on Tupperware boxes, in order to make sure that her family stays away from the golden arches while she's gone. Mothers of young children might stress about what their children wear, and indeed, I have sometimes seen the odd official playschool photo with a little princess wearing a frilly dress, rubber boots and a tiara – daddy got her ready for the photo shoot. The best way to avoid this, then, is to lay out all the clothes in the order that they should be worn, and with written guidelines on which items and colors can be combined... We do have the habit of writing long lists on how to organize the children and their hobbies while "Mummy taxi" is away. What to do when Child A's soccer game overlaps with Child B's dance class on the other side of town, and how to get Child C to her art class on time... and so on.

LEAVING HOME

Grab your trolley bag and smiling lips,
fill your pockets with euros and dollars,
lip gloss and high heels
– a trip somewhere
and endless friendliness.

Run from the changing room
and into the briefing room,
remember your CIS brief
* and equipment checklists,*
change float and special meals,
finally the security control
* and line for the crew bus,*
hurry up the stairs and
– Welcome!

Counting heads
again and again
– Are you ready?
– Where can I put these?
– Check the seatbelts!

Are you ready –
Finally gathering speed
– Take your positions!

Sirpa Kivilaakso

"I FORGOT THE MILK! AND WAS I SUPPOSED TO BAKE SOMETHING?"

I sometimes feel I have done a full day's work before even getting to the airport car park. Then it's time for last messages home, like "I forgot the milk! Could you buy some?" While dragging your trolley bag to the crew center you might remember that it's parent-teacher meeting night at school, and you were perhaps supposed to bake something for it.

Coming home is the best part about going away – that feeling, when the wheels touch the ground at Helsinki-Vantaa Airport, and you know that you will soon be able to open your own front door. Not everyone lives right next to the airport, though, and some of us have a long drive

home; how to stay awake after a night flight? A few even have to catch a flight to get home.

The joy of being back does include a few tricky moments, at least for those of us, who have someone waiting at home. How many of us have come back from a long flight and sworn to be happy and patient, and to not start nagging the second we walk in? Unfortunately, there is a fair chance that you might indeed have a temper tantrum on arrival. After all, nothing will cheer you up like a stack of pizza boxes in the hall, blocking the door so that you can barely get in, while all the food you lovingly cooked before leaving has remained untouched. The target of your affections, your teenage son, is lying on the couch in a half-coma, grasping his Playstation controls, and nobody appears to have remembered to take the trash out for a couple of days. Suitcases tend to land with a loud thump in those situations. Exactly where did that euphoric feeling of being back go? "So, how have you been? Oh, you forgot about car-pooling, and the milk? And you've been eating pizza for three days, yeah, I noticed! Isn't that just fantastic!" It's probably not the first or last time that after that long night-walk over Siberia, you might end up saying a whole lot more than you intended.

A flight attendant classic is to go and visit your local grocery store in your uniform on your way home, in order to avoid giving that "So you forgot to buy groceries" sermon to your family as soon as you walk through the door. And you just know they would have forgotten to buy toilet paper. Sometimes you're just feeling too tired and fragile to be

Photo by: Cabin Crew Peter Fagerström

using paper napkins left over from last Christmas, or that cheap and scratchy kitchen roll that your husband has a habit of buying.

I have heard that a colleague once mowed the lawn in her uniform, straight after a night flight, much to her neighbors' amazement. "Humph, I see nobody's cut the grass. Fine, I might as well do it while I still have some energy left, so that I can then relax!" Her husband also woke up to the noise and looked out, rubbing his eyes. "Oh, how nice that you're back."

Another colleague told me that her neighbor had stopped to ask if she was feeling ok. She had parked her car and was lifting her suitcase out, when she noticed that the cardboard bin was overflowing. Still in her uniform, she pulled on a pair of rubber boots and climbed in to flatten the boxes. The sight of a flight attendant jumping up and down in a waste bin on a Sunday morning had struck the neighbor as somewhat odd behavior. I guess he'd just moved into the neighborhood.

CREW STORIES

 AS I WAS leaving for work, I noticed my neighbor waving urgently. I stopped the car and asked what the matter was. "Your handbag is on the roof of the car."

 I'M A FREELANCE writer, and I happened to be working on a very important article, when I had to leave for a three-day trip. My biggest concern was that my house might be burgled while I was gone, so I needed to put my laptop in a safe place. Now, if you were a burglar, where might you not look? The oven, of course! When I returned, I was pleased to notice that my house had not been broken into, but I was hungry, and there was no food, save for a frozen pizza. I switched the oven on and hopped in the shower. The smell of burning plastic soon brought on a flashback about putting my laptop in the oven, and I hurried to salvage my writing. With the help of a "collector of hot data" that I new, I discovered that a computer hard disc can survive temperatures up to 65 Celsius degrees, but heating the disc is still not recommended in any way.

 AS I WAS leaving home very early in the morning, for the fourth morning in a row, I was about to lock the front door when I noticed that the entire lock was gone. It took me about 15 seconds to realize that I had only shut the interior door.

"LOOK MUMMY, WE'RE EVACUATING!"

✈ **I WAS LEAVING** for a flight and my son was playing in the backyard with his nanny and the neighborhood "sandbox troops". "Hey, hey mummy! Bring pressies!" he shouted after me. "No dear," I replied, "I'm not going anywhere I can shop, and I'll be back tonight!" "Well, then bring pie!" At the time, Fazer's berry pies were served on all European routes, and I often brought mine home for the children. Once again, the neighbors had a good laugh.

✈ **WHEN MY SONS** were still young, I was working as a safety instructor. Children tend to be very attentive, and, as a result, I suppose my children were not entirely unfamiliar with my field of expertise. The boys raised some eyebrows at the playground, when they shouted at the top of the slide, "Look, mummy, we're evacuating!"

✈ **I WAS GOING** back to work part time after several years at home, and my oldest daughter was about to start at much-awaited pre-school. "Mummy, are you sure they've processed my application for part-time pre-school?"

✈ **I OFTEN TELL** my family what lovely colleagues I have. During the presidential elections, I told my three-year-old that I was going to go and vote. "I'm voting for the crew too. I just love them!" He said, with a big, sunny smile on his face.

PLANS CHANGE

Recently, there was an article in Newsweek about Steward Ron Akawi, age 83. Hawaiian-born Ron applied for a job with United Airlines in 1949, in order to get to go to Los Angeles, just once. Ron's dream came true – he got to see Los Angeles many, many times, and has been flying with United for over 60 years!

Summer jobs with Finnair have also ended up lasting decades. The world has become smaller as aircraft have become faster, and flight schedules today are calculated by the minute. The goal of every airline is to get their passengers to their destinations safely and on schedule.

Pre-flight procedures are carefully planned and executed. Flight attendants have to carry out their duties in a calm manner but within a very short time, abiding by regulations and instructions. Occasionally, something unexpected will happen and change the entire course of the flight.

IT WAS 23 December in Beijing. Our aircraft was taxiing towards the runway. The cabin was ready for takeoff, and we were at our duty stations, waiting for the captain's announcement, "Cabin crew, please be seated for takeoff." In addition to safety-related duties, I am sure that each of us was thinking about Christmas, which in Finland is celebrated already on the 24th. I would have time to slip little presents into the children's Christmas stockings before they woke up… We stood still, waited, and glanced at each other a little nervously as the engines roared and quieted down again. Passengers were getting a little restless, which increased as the captain announced, "Ladies and

gentlemen, unfortunately we are experiencing some technical difficulties and have to return to the gate…" So much for a peaceful Christmas Eve then. We pushed back the thought of our waiting families, and began answering customers' queries as well as we could, which at that point was not very well. "I'm sorry, we have no further information about the length of the delay… We'll let you know as soon as we hear something." We returned to the gate, greeted by a group of technical staff. Passengers disembarked to wait inside the terminal. After some time we heard that fixing the aircraft would take nearly 24 hours, and most of our passengers would be rerouted. We waited in Beijing, and eventually got home long after Santa had come and gone.

MISHAPS IN NEW YORK

✈ AN ORDINARY DAY in Finland: We started our walk over the Atlantic with the intention of being in New York in the afternoon. Just as we were about to begin our approach to JFK Airport, the airport was shut down due to a blizzard, and all air traffic was diverted. We landed at an army airfield, which naturally had poor facilities for commercial traffic, and no immigration or customs authorities. More and more aircraft landed, and apparently there were some negotiations going on, whether to send the required authorities to us, or to wait for JFK to reopen. Passengers were getting a little restless, when we finally

received information that JFK would reopen soon. Unfortunately, since we had been the first to arrive, we were parked in a corner, and were then the last to leave. The blizzard at JFK was a source of mirth to anyone who has been born and bred in the Nordic countries: there was barely 20 cm of snow on the ground! We then had to wait for our arrival gate to vacate, but there were apparently only two push-back tractors in use at the entire airport, so it took quite a long time. We finally got to our gate, but then there were problems with the passenger bridge. More waiting. When even the last passenger had disembarked, we let out a sigh of great relief – but too soon!

Inside the terminal, there were problems with the luggage conveyor belts; they kept getting stuck, and bringing snow inside. There was no sign of our crew bags. A member of the ground staff told us that the tail loader was broken. I don't know how they got our luggage down (free fall?), but a few suitcases looked like they had suffered a few knocks. Our transportation to the hotel had been cancelled due to the weather. The queue for taxis was almost as long as the trip to Manhattan. After we had waited a little longer (!), the ground handling agent miraculously managed to get us "one of the two buses that were actually running that day". Thank you. The airport was in total chaos. When we finally got on the bus, we again let out a sigh of relief, and even laughed a little. We were still not able to leave, however, because a car had caught fire in the parking lot, and the fire brigade arrived, stopping all traffic for a while… Eventually we did manage to leave the airport, but were not able to get to Manhattan on our first attempt, as there had been an accident and the Midtown tunnel was closed. We had to take a detour over Queensborough Bridge, which was close to shutting down as well, since the road was now dangerously slippery. To add to the excitement, our bus-driver was not used to driving a stick-shift vehicle and the bus had summer tires. We did finally make it to the hotel. A lesson learned: the length of your work day is not always what it says on your roster. I think it's remarkable that we have cold, long winters in Finland, and Helsinki-Vantaa Airport still runs like clockwork. Thank you, ground staff, you do an amazing job with your "snow how"!

UNDER THE ASH CLOUD

 ROSTER: MORNING FLIGHT to Manchester; back in the afternoon. I had the flu, and had to stay home, meaning that a colleague would be called out from standby to operate the flight. I was in no condition to fly, but still felt guilty – my replacement would only have two hours to get to the airport... Then again, the flight would be back in the afternoon, early enough for her/him to pick up the kids from daycare... I switched on the news: Volcanic ash cloud drifts over Europe. Airports were shutting down, first London Heathrow, and then Manchester! Gosh, I would have been stuck there if I didn't have the flu! My replacement was indeed stuck – first at the airport for a few hours, and then at a hotel for days. The crew eventually got home by train, bus and ship; first through the Channel tunnel and into France, then Paris, Hamburg, Copenhagen, Gothenburg, Stockholm and finally Helsinki. Finnair crew members were picked up from destinations along the way, and their stories of ash cloud complications included everything under the sun, from dog-sitter arrangements to wedding cancellations. While Europe was waiting for the sky to clear, I had had time to recover from the flu. I was scheduled for a flight to Hong Kong just after Helsinki-Vantaa Airport had reopened. I was ready to leave the house when I received notification that the wind had changed direction and my flight was cancelled. Instead of Hong Kong, I was needed on a flight to Bangkok leaving on the same day. Minutes later, I was informed that Helsinki-Vantaa Airport had to close down again, and our flight would leave from Tampere instead. The company had hired a bus to take us to Tampere. There were several other flight crews on the bus. On the way, we heard that Tampere Airport would have to shut down too, and the closest airport that was functioning now was in Kuopio. We must have had that ash cloud right above us, because Kuopio Airport closed before we got there. Our caravan, consisting of our bus and the catering truck, continued its journey towards Oulu. We arrived in Oulu at the crack of dawn, already 10 hours of duty time behind us. We opted to operate the flight anyway. The catering lift was not working, so we ended up carrying all the trolleys and other equipment on board the aircraft. We landed in Bangkok approximately 24 hours after our departure from Helsinki. We were happy in spite of our exhaustion, as our efforts ensured that other colleagues and passengers could finally start their journey home!

CHAPTER 5

BEFORE TAKEOFF

THE HEART OF the Crew Center, the Crew Service Desk (CSD), is probably the most understanding entity for flight attendants, right after their own families. CSD personnel are always ready to help us, just like catering and technical staff. CSD will offer a helping hand in any last-minute changes regarding flights, and for example, send reminders about travel documents that are about to expire. One could call them flight attendants' foster mommies, and just like mothers, they will kiss our boo-boos, nod understandingly when we stumble, and rejoice with us, when we finally learn how to stand on our own feet. Just like mothers, they know a lot more than they admit, and will draw conclusions about the rest, just from the click-clack of our high heels. Sometimes we tend to forget that mothers are there to support us, not do our pirouettes for us. Here are a few examples of where that support should end and our own initiative begin:

- On a Saturday morning, a very apologetic flight attendant called, saying that she was rather pathetic at reading a map, and could I give her directions to IKEA?

- A flight attendant was skiing in Lapland with a colleague, who had fallen and injured herself. Should she call the insurance company, and which one, did I know?

- A steward was skating and had a head-on collision with his friend. Could he come to work with a black eye? Another colleague had suggested he should come in ask his supervisor's opinion…

- "Since you know everything… I bought this salad dressing for a colleague from Japan last time – you wouldn't happen to know what that dressing is called?

● The phone rang in the evening. "Finnair Health Services has closed for the day, and I need to see a doctor. Where should I go?"

● A steward came to the CSD saying that he'd forgotten his uniform shoes at home. He said he was wearing black sneakers, and could work in those, if it was ok with the rest of the crew. I leaned out to have a look. The sneakers had broad white stripes on them and white shoelaces.

● A flight attendant called from her holiday trip to Paris. "Which terminal do we use here? So much easier to leave from here, if I know which terminal to go to."

● I was once asked to call a repairman for household appliances…

● A pilot once asked us to reimburse a one-euro payment for parking, which he had to pay while picking up his visa at the U.S. Embassy.

● On Midsummer Eve, a flight attendant called to ask if I knew of a medical center in Hämeen-linna that might be open, since she was just on her way there…

● A flight attendant called to say that she was going on holiday to Boston, and did I know if under-aged children needed some sort of travel documents?

"IT'S FUN TO PLAY CUPID"

● A man called, asking for a flight attendant's phone number. I wasn't allowed to give it, of course, but I told him that I could pass on the message. The man poured his heart out; she had been on his flight,

TWILIGHT ON MONTMARTRE

I step on to Paris twilight at Montmartre.

*On my way
The Pompidou opened its tube:
  sucked in a fire-eater
I an oyster
on top of a red-and-white
  checkered cloth
and
in that moment felt
the thunder of the ocean
  and sharpness of the blue.*

Sirpa Kivilaakso

and now he was thinking about her all the time, and couldn't get any work done. I called the flight attendant, told her about the man, and she gave me permission to give her phone number to him. She seemed quite taken by him too. It's fun to play Cupid.

- The thousand dollar question: "What do they serve at the '20 years of service' buffet?"

- The captain of a Tokyo flight called to say that a passenger's glasses had been crushed inside a business class seat. The passenger was heading on a 10-day business trip to Riga, and was now as blind as a bat. The purser thought that we should contact her supervisor and try to get her to replace the glasses somehow. What a magical moment it would be, if the glasses would be waiting for him, when he arrived in Helsinki! Sure, customers are our top priority too, but...

- A flight attendant called and said that she was going to Korea for the first time, and was wondering where to find information concerning the currency and other important matters. I suggested that she could try Google.

- A flight attendant called from the aircraft and said that she couldn't find any portion milk onboard, but there was a large milk carton and a milk jug. Should she give passengers extra milk from the jug then?

- "Hey, could you call the ID Ticket Office or e-mail them and ask how I could get to Toronto in the winter, and how much it might cost?"

- Steward: "I'm gonna be a little late, because this bus is like... one of those."
CSD: "One of what?"
Steward: "You know... One of those that stops all the time."
To myself: Well, you didn't think to take an earlier bus then? Surely it's not that unusual for buses to pick up and drop off passengers?

- "I'm never there during the airport laundry opening hours. Could someone drop off my shirts?"

- "There's a sample for the health services in my mailbox. Could someone drop it off for me?"

- And finally: "Could someone lend me five euros?"

To Finnair flight crew, Crew Control is the invisible nerve centre controlling their lives, and many other things too. They perform impossible feats the equivalent of balancing on a tightrope with a unicycle while juggling burning torches, whistling the "Ride of the Valkyries" and dodging pendulums hanging from the ceiling. In reality they monitor several computer screens, solve mysteries of ever-altering data, and have become used to nasty surprises. Every flight is built like a jigsaw puzzle, and it is the Crew Control's duty to ensure that all the pieces are in place: an adequate number of pilots and cabin crew with the right qualifications on the right flights. Sometimes they even seem to pull out aircraft from their sleeve.

CREW STORIES

THE STYLISH AND immaculately groomed flight attendant that I am, I had, once again, left home in the morning in a bit of a hurry. I wore trousers on the flight, and was wondering during the service why my left thigh felt odd, like there was a lump or something extra in the trouser leg. Once I was back in the galley, I noticed that not only was a pair of pantyhose stuck in a heap inside my trousers, but also, the tip of one leg was sticking out and dragging behind me. My colleagues fell apart laughing, as I pulled the pantyhose out like a magician pulling scarves from his hat. To this day, I wonder how I and everyone else on the flight had failed to notice my odd appendage until then.

I WAS CALLED out from standby and had to leave in a rush. I had pulled my pantyhose on the wrong way, so that the heel and toe reinforcements were on the top of my feet. I didn't notice that anything was wrong until the very end of the flight. A colleague revealed that she had noticed, but thought that I was wearing some kind of ankle brace, and decided not to say anything.

MAGICIANS GUIDING US IN THE SKY

AN EARLY MORNING flight to Stockholm. The computers at the crew center had crashed, so instead of signing in for work, I called Crew Control. Everything went according to plan, until the captain walked up to me in Stockholm and asked if I was on the correct flight. "Yes, of course I am," I replied. "It says Stockholm on my roster." "Hm… Ok, I don't know, but Crew Control just called to check." Once I got to Helsinki and switched my cell phone on, I noticed that Crew Control had attempted to get in touch with me, and had left a message asking me to call back. Oh dear! I called them and asked with a shaky voice, "Was I on the wrong flight?" "Yes, you were," the controller replied. "Don't you remember, when you called in the morning, I asked you to go to Kajaani instead, and you said ok." Who me? I had no recol-

lection of doing anything of the sort. Fortunately, Crew Control had managed to get another flight attendant for the flight to Kajaani.

 CREW CONTROL CALLED me on my day off to ask if I could do a favor and do the flight to Beijing that day. "Sure," I replied, helpful as I am. "I have one condition, though." "What?" the controller asked. "That I can dead head both ways." "Er, how come?" asked the controller. "I'm no longer qualified for the MD-11..." That call ended rather abruptly, as the controller needed to find someone else quickly. I would have gladly gone, but of course, heads would have rolled had I attempted to work onboard an aircraft I was not qualified for.

ONE OF THE flight controllers told me that he once got a rather odd call on his night shift: "Hi, this is Steward X calling from Hong Kong... Er, can you tell me which hotel we stay at these days?"

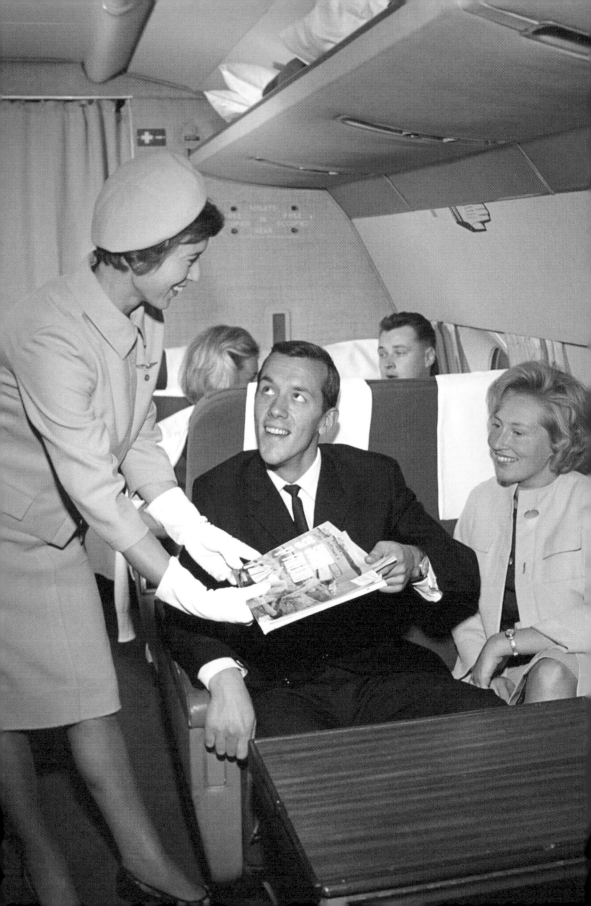

CHAPTER 6

CRUISE

WHAT MAKES A flight "a good flight"? For one passenger, the flight is preparation for an important presentation. For another, being able to concentrate on writing a report on the conference he just attended. A third is going on holiday and wants to party. The fourth is travelling but he'd rather be at home, and the fifth just wants to block out the noise and be left alone, eyes closed and ears plugged. As cabin crew, we need to accommodate all of these needs.

Safety is a top priority. Motivated and highly trained personnel assess risks every day in aircraft maintenance, in the cockpit, cabin, air traffic control tower, cargo, and departure gate. Any lapses, and especially any failures, will soon be noticed. Some mistakes can be made only once.

Another dimension for assessing a good flight is punctuality regarding the flight itself, as well as other services. Our target is to always be on schedule, but there are many variables that we have no control over.

The atmosphere among the crew is infectious, and will affect everyone in the cabin. It is just so much easier to breathe around people who are in a good mood.

Safety and punctuality are taken for granted, and they can be verified by statistics and graphs. Atmosphere can only be measured on an emotional

THE FLIGHT ATTENDANT'S WORK DAY

- Good morning, how are you?
- Through the galley
  and to your right, please

A leisure flight from the Canaries
  bringing Tom, Dick and Harry
  and a red-faced Lisa
  back into the cold.
-Through the galley
    and to your right, please
  Meatballs for lunch
  Oh, how wonderful!
  Finnish coffee!

- Where are we now?
- How long did you get to stay?
- Make mine a double!
- Are you always on this same route?

How wonderful.

Sirpa Kivilaakso

level. Different people have different needs, and being the chameleons that we are, most of the time we can meet those needs.

The following stories are pickings from years of funny and surprising situations on flights. Certain situations are only funny afterwards, and in some cases, we had to keep our amusement to ourselves. These stories are small samples of the chemistry people have and how it often manifests as situational comedy at 30,000 feet.

CREW STORIES

SOMETIMES PLANS CHANGE quickly. My crew was supposed to continue to Oulu after a European flight, which turned out to be delayed. There was a deadheading crew on the same flight, and in order to make up for some lost time, Crew Control changed the status of the deadheading crew to operating crew, so that all pre-flight preparations could be completed on time, and the flight would stay on schedule. Imagine our surprise, when we got to the departure gate, and saw the Oulu flight taking off! The others had not been informed that we were on our way. We were to fly back with the aircraft and new passengers from Oulu, and the deadheading crew (now operating), were to stay in Oulu for the night. We were desperately needed, so the aircraft had to turn back and pick us up. A rather embarrassing mistake, but it makes for a good story- after all, not everybody gets picked up for work with an aircraft...

A YOUNG FIRST officer came onboard, and began to list what he wanted to eat. "Could I have tea with lemon, some porridge with a dollop of butter, not too watery, a crew sandwich, a coke, some orange juice, and blueberry soup now, and my hot meal pretty soon after takeoff?" Now, I believe that sometimes words aren't needed, so I said, "Uhuh... hang on, let me get my colleague." I got the other steward, an old friend of mine, from the rear galley. "Ok, I'm here, can you repeat that for me?" The first officer repeated his long list, to our great amusement. We smiled and nodded. "Can you believe this guy?" I chuckled, and walked away.

THE MONEYMAN

IT WAS THE end of the Soviet era, and Russian citizens were finally issued permits to travel abroad. I remember one Sergei, who walked down the passenger bridge, threw his bag down at my feet, and announced, in an excited tone, "I am rich!"

WE HAD TO pick up some passengers with a DC-9 from Pori and take them to a destination in Europe. There had just been a small blunder in Helsinki, and the aircraft had full tanks. The Pori Airport has such a short runway that we would not be able to take off safely, and there was no equipment to suck the fuel out of the tanks. What to do? We noticed that there was a group of 30 children coming on board, and they were, of course, lighter than average adult passengers. The solution: we weighed the children, so that the red cap could calculate the actual weight of the aircraft. In addition, the engines were revved for another 10 minutes before departure to burn up some extra fuel, and we managed to take off safely. I've not had the need to weigh passengers since.

THE RED CAP (or RC) was a profession that no longer exists. Red Caps were responsible for aircraft balance calculations, and coordinated everything else to do with the flight: special passengers, cargo, refueling, catering. Nowadays, we call the department we need directly with the aircraft cell phone.

OUR CAPTAIN RECEIVED an urgent message when he was already in the cockpit, and had to go back home. The passengers were already onboard, and we had to wait about an hour and a half until the captain's replacement arrived. An elderly couple was getting impatient: "Finnair should offer us some free brandy – or the captain should at least apologize!" I listened silently for as long as I could, but eventually said, "The captain received some very bad news from home, and had to leave. I'm sure you understand that an apology was not first and foremost on his mind."

BEFORE THE NEW terminal building had even been built at Helsinki-Vantaa, Convair aircraft were often parked at a remote stand, which meant that the passengers had a long walk across the tarmac (buses were not in use at the time). One November day, the weather was dreadful: snow and sleet was falling from the sky, with a biting wind to heighten the misery. As I stood at the aircraft door, nearly every passenger made a comment about the weather, or complained that we had parked too far from the terminal. I assumed that all passengers were already onboard, but peeked out to make sure, when I noticed a young man in a short-sleeved shirt slowly walking towards the plane. He must have just arrived from somewhere warm. I grabbed a couple of blankets for him, thinking he would need them, but he happily skipped up the steps and said, "Not a single mosquito. I love it!"

WE WERE BOARDING a leisure flight in Rhodes, and I was standing at the door to greet passengers. A Finnish couple, both topless, was walking up the stairs. I might be a bit old-fashioned, but I think that what's appropriate for the beach isn't necessarily so for a flight. "Could I kindly suggest that you put some more clothes on?" I asked in a friendly tone. No response. After two more attempts I finally raised my voice, "Put your tops on or stay here!" The couple did find something decent to wear, but not entirely without complaint, "Finns are so narrow-minded and intolerant."

A MEMBER OF our ground staff in Singapore once observed that he feels privileged in being able to send people from Sin to Hel.

 I ONCE HAD the pleasure of seeing a man embark on a leisure flight wearing a cycling helmet. I assumed that he would take it off once he had settled into his seat and found a place for his things, but no. Halfway into the flight, I plucked up the courage to ask if he perhaps wanted me to put the helmet in the overhead locker. "Oh no, thank you. I prefer to keep it on in case of an emergency."

"WHAT DO I HAVE TO SAY TO GET A BEER?"

 WE SERVE PASSENGERS in three to four different languages, so it's only natural that we sometimes get confused. Once, I just could not make out what a foreign-looking passenger was saying, and, blushing, asked for the third time in English, "I'm sorry; I didn't catch that... what would you like to drink?" He replied in perfect Finnish but in a rather annoyed tone, "What do I have to say to get a beer?"

 A MIDDLE-AGED COUPLE was traveling to a destination in Asia, but had been late to check in and hadn't managed to get seats together. The man was upset, and began a one-man there's-no way-I'm-putting-up-with-this show. He insisted they get seats together, and since economy class was full, he believed they were entitled to an upgrade. At this point, he was snapping his fingers flamenco-style, which really does not help, as anyone working in customer service could tell you. The purser decided to upgrade two elderly ladies, who were heading for a long-awaited dream holiday, and gave their original seats to the couple. For some reason, the man didn't seem that happy, even though he got what he had wanted – a seat next to his wife. The cabin crew also noticed that the couple did not speak a word to each other on the entire 10-hour flight. A love shared but unspoken, perhaps?

🥂 **A UN PEACEKEEPERS'** flight to Pristina: The Colonel walked in and told me that he had had a word with his men and they all agreed that there would be no need for inflight entertainment, as they had seen the films in our selection already. "Fine," I replied. At the beginning of the flight, however, I decided to make an announcement, "Gentlemen, since you're not interested in our DVD selection, does anyone have a good film of your own that we could all watch with the aircraft system?" I peeked into the cabin, to see about 100 grinning faces. "Gentlemen, I did mean a film that we can actually show in public!"

🥂 **ON A LEISURE** flight to the Canaries two elderly ladies complained repeatedly about how uncomfortable the seats were. "When will you fix these?" one of them asked. "On Thursday," I replied. "Oh thank you!" the ladies gushed.

🥂 **IN THE OLD** days, we used to buy designer watches at Amsterdam Airport and Cartier rings in Berlin. I had bought a watch with a light brown leather strap and a white face decorated with Chinese letters. I had worn it for a couple of months, when suddenly on a

Frankfurt flight a passenger offered to buy it. I had already declined several times, until I finally said, as a joke, "You can have it for a 1,000." I had paid 170 marks for it. The passenger pulled out a 1,000-mark note from his shirt pocket, so what could I do? I gave him the watch and took the money. Once I got home I backed my car into the mailbox in my driveway and the steel edge scraped it so badly that it cost 2,000 marks to fix. Easy come, easy go.

I'M WELL ACQUAINTED with Japanese protocol and politeness, but as I was serving welcome drinks in business class, I stepped on the toes of an elderly Japanese gentleman and lost my balance. I landed in his lap with my hand in his groin. "Hoo!" said the man. "Haw!" exclaimed his wife. I backed into the galley bowing so low that my forehead practically touched the floor. To my surprise, the couple was amused, and for the rest of the flight, started laughing every time I approached them.

"YOU'RE MY HOMEBOYS, AREN'T YOU?"

FINNAIR CARRIES APPROXIMATELY eight million passengers a year, so it's no surprise if we sometimes confuse the faces of people we know and people we think we know...

ONCE, ON A domestic flight perhaps 20 years ago, I recognized one of the passengers, a man approximately my own age. "We went to the same school, didn't we?" No? Perhaps he was from my hometown, or we had worked somewhere together… Summer camp? Eventually a steward pulled me away and hissed, "Would you quit already! It's the champion ski jumper, Jari Puikkonen!" "Ah, I didn't quite recognize him without his helmet, but there was definitely something familiar!" I exclaimed, laughing. Fortunately, the ski jumper was amused too.

Annually, Finnair carries a passenger load nearly double the population of Finland, so it is no wonder that occasionally one is unable to distinguish between acquaintances, familiar faces, and people one actually knows.

A FEW YEARS ago, I was called from standby to operate a flight to Bangkok. The call came quite late, so I missed the pre-flight briefing and went straight to the aircraft. We started boarding almost as soon as I got there, and I stood at door L3 greeting passengers. When nearly everyone was onboard, I noticed a young man, who looked familiar, walking down the aisle. I said a friendly hello, thinking that he must be my cousin's boyfriend, whom I'd met only once before. He was equally friendly in his reply. I still wasn't quite sure if it really was him, so I went to talk to him when I had the chance. "You look really familiar," I said. "Yeah, so do you," he replied smiling. I thought that the manner he replied in was a bit odd (especially if he was my cousin's boyfriend!), so I decided to investigate further. Was he not from Haukiputaa? And apparently not my cousin's boyfriend? How strange, considering he looked so familiar and all. Bemused, I went back to the galley and explained what had just happened to my colleague. "That's Jere Hård, the swimmer!" she said. "We have the whole national swim team onboard – did you not hear that at the briefing?" Oh no! I was so embarrassed; I had to go back one more time and apologize for being so intrusive. He just laughed it off, thank heavens.

A COUPLE I knew walked in and sat close to my duty station. We talked for a while, but I just could not place them. How did I know these people? Could they be friends of my parents? Or the parents or grandparents of my children's friends? I just couldn't remember, and eventually I had to ask how we knew each other. "You brought us back from Rhodes a couple of weeks ago," the woman replied. Oh, of course! Good thing I hadn't revealed any dark secrets or my innermost thoughts…

THIS HAPPENED BACK in the 1980s on a flight from Helsinki to Madrid via Athens. The aircraft was a Super Caravelle, which had a first class and an economy class. The passengers continuing to Madrid stayed onboard in Athens. We had some time to spare on the ground, so I walked up to the forward galley. The curtain between the galley and first class was closed. "I learnt this hilarious song yesterday," I told the steward working in first class. "Let's hear it!" he said. The song was a bit dirty, and told the story of an American soldier putting the moves on his girl. The first verse began, "This is number one, and the fun has just begun…" I amused my colleague by singing all of the nine verses, and then headed back to my duty station for boarding. A first class passenger called me to his seat sternly. "Yes sir?" "There's a tenth verse, you know, and it goes like this: Now, this is number ten, and he's started once again… and the song is called Roll Me Over." Moral of the story: galley curtains are not sound proof.

"SO, IS THAT AN EJECTION SEAT?"

BACK IN THE day, we served spirits from large bottles on double drink trolleys. The tomato juice was in a pitcher at the other end of the trolley, and I asked my colleague to pass it to me. I reached for it, but somehow lost my grip, and the next thing I knew was that a British gentleman wearing a beige suit was fully covered in tomato juice. What could I do, except say how incredibly sorry I was, and try and clean him up? I felt so bad I had to fight back tears as I wiped his glasses windshield wiper-style with a napkin. It turned out the passenger was a professor, who would only be in Helsinki for one day to give a lecture, and didn't have a change of clothes with him. It was clear he wouldn't be able to attend any event looking as he did. The pilots contacted Helsinki, and managed to arrange for a new suit for the professor – the ground staff delivered it to our arrival gate. The professor left the aircraft wrapped in Finnair blankets, and nobody could bring themselves to utter the usually so neutral "Have a nice day!"

AN ELDERLY COUPLE sat opposite my jumpseat on the DC-10. The woman had not been onboard an aircraft before, and asked all kinds of questions. When I sat down for takeoff, pulled on my gloves and tightened the safety harness, she asked, "So, is that what they call an ejection seat?"

A jump seat is a folding seat with a four-point safety harness. The cabin crew sits on these seats for takeoff and landing.

A BUSINESS CLASS passenger on a long-haul flight looked at me from top to toe. I suppose you could say he undressed me with his eyes, and then said, "I don't like you. I want somebody else to serve me!"

 FLIGHT ATTENDANT: "WOULD you like an aperitif?"
Passenger: "Yes."
Flight attendant: "What would you like?"
Passenger: "An aperitif, like you suggested!"
Flight attendant: "Yes, so what would you like to have?"
Passenger: "The *aperitif*, like I said!"

 PASSENGER: "I'D LIKE to have a soft drink."
Flight attendant: "Coke, Fanta or Sprite?"
Passenger: "No, a *soft drink*!"

A FINNISH PASSENGER ordered "A scotch on the rocks." As I was putting the ice in his glass, he yelled, "No, no ice!"

WE USED TO serve Beaujolais Nouveau. I recommended it to a nice couple, and explained that it was a special kind of wine, as it was made from that year's harvest, and not aged. "Well, do you happen to have older Beaujolais we could try, so that we could compare the two?"

I WAS WORKING in business class on my first or second European flight ever. I didn't think to open the bottle of sparkling water beforehand in the galley, but did it on the aisle, and of course the contents emptied like F1 winner's champagne, spraying all over an ex-politician, who was known as a man of few words. I apologized profusely, but could not get a smile or a word out of him for the entire flight.

I WAS SERVING drinks on a flight to Paris, and when I got to an elderly couple, the man already had a firm grip on a 20-euro note he'd pulled out from his wallet. "No need," I said. "This is a scheduled flight and all beverages are complimentary." "Well, in that case! Give one for the wife as well!" the man replied. I made hers a double.

PASSENGERS OCCASIONALLY ASK for all kinds of exotic juices, like guava, kiwi fruit, or mango. I usually reply politely that "Mangoes are not in season in Finland right now."

DING! CALL BELL. "Yes?" I ask the passenger. He is Swedish, and wants a neat whisky. I take it to him, and as soon as I'm back in the galley, there's another "ding" from his seat. "Yes?" "Listen, this whiskey is way too strong!"

"BEST TRIP EVER!"

ON A FLIGHT to London sometime in the 1980s, I was lifting a pitcher of orange juice, when it slipped from my hand and spilled all over a musician sitting in the aisle seat. I froze on the spot, and for some reason my colleague mumbled, "You need to apologize and give him 50 marks." Everyone seemed to hold their breath for a while, but the victim was the first to start laughing. The situation was completely absurd: a steward was laughing with his head inside a cupboard, another flight attendant was doubled up in the galley, the victim and the rest of his orchestra were holding their stomachs and guffawing loudly, and one of the flight attendants was still repeating, "You need to apologize and give him 50 marks." The passenger only wanted a beer. He was in a good mood, returning home after a successful tour. "Best flight ever!" he said, leaving the aircraft in London. Everyone else on board appeared to agree.

A SMALL, BALD and wrinkly American man, who must have been over 80 years old, asked me with a shaky voice if we had any tomato juice. "Sure!" I replied. "I'll have a glass of that, please, and you should have one too!" I asked why, and he replied, "It's good for your prostate," he said, pointing at his groin. "I'll take your word for it, sir, but I don't have any problems with mine." The old man grinned and remarked, "Oh, but you will, son. You will!"

ON A LEISURE flight, a rather well-marinated man asked for another drink. My colleague, a rather brash steward, activated his "breathalyzer" (the Fly Top), and asked the passenger to blow. The passenger did so, but bad luck for him, the red light came on to indicate that he had had too many drinks already. The rest of us had a hard time keeping a straight face, but the steward played his role well – and no wonder, as he had been trained as a policeman.

🥂 **A COLLEAGUE ASKED** me if I could make a whisky soda and take it to the passenger in 10 A. I took the drink to the passenger, but she was an old lady, and had not asked for anything, neither had anyone else around her. I went back to the galley. My colleague racked her brain for a while, and then realized that someone had asked her for a whisky soda on her previous flight – the day before! Better late than never.

On flights, all sales are registered into POS (point-of-sale) terminals. The first one we had onboard was called Fly Top, and the current device is known as Mobbe. The Fly Top had a barcode reader with a red light, which could be activated by pressing a button.

🥂 **I ACCIDENTALLY SPILT** a little tomato juice on a male passenger. I helped him clean his shirt, and offered him some champagne after apologizing several times for what had happened. The woman sitting next to him said that she had a few drops on her dress as well, so I performed the same "champagne and clean up routine" for her. Soon the couple asked for more drinks, and I asked if they were celebrating something special. The couple said that they had only just met, and probably only started talking because of the juice incident. They disembarked together, with some clearly romantic chemistry between them. I don't know if the relationship lasted beyond the arrival hall, but I certainly felt better about my mishap.

🥂 **I HAD REPEATEDLY** told a middle-aged male passenger that it was forbidden to drink one's own alcohol onboard, and would confiscate the bottle if he didn't stop right away. As he disembarked, he gave me a murderous look and said I'd be better off quitting, since I was so "old and stale".

"REPEAT MY WIFE"

THERE WAS TIME, when we didn't charge for spirits. I was walking along the aisle, when a tall Russian man put his hand up in front of me and said, "Stoi." I stopped. "One ganyak." I got the bottle and a glass and poured him the drink. As a grand gesture, he pointed at the woman next to him and said, "Repeat my wife."

FLIGHTS TO AND from Moscow in the 1980s were somewhat wilder than today. Alcohol was free and flowed freely, but still many felt that they were not getting their drinks quickly enough. Being the practical people that we are, we tried to come up with a solution with the crew. We toyed with several ideas, but this is what I remember the best: When you check in for your flight, you would be asked whether you wanted to have vodka, gin, whisky, cognac or rum during the flight, and you would be seated accordingly. The oxygen generators above the seats would be replaced with alcohol containers, and the straws would be dropped down after takeoff, and reeled back in for landing. Genius! However, we never passed the idea forward, as we suspected the aviation authorities might have a thing or two to say about our plan.

I WAS SERVING drinks with a colleague, who had a similar hairstyle to mine, but we had very little else in common. Two little old ladies were going on holiday together, and one of them asked if we were sisters. "No, we're not," answered my colleague. "Ah, twins then?" asked the other.

IT WAS ONE of those "company recreation week in Lapland" flights, with maybe an hour to serve passengers and a full plane. The flight was full of groups from various companies, and typically one member of the group would pay for all the drinks. The problem was that the group members were split up all over the plane.

Engineer 1: "Can we get nine cognacs, please!"

Engineer 2 (sitting next to him): "No, we're 11!"

Engineer 3 from the other side of the aisle: "I don't drink cognac, I want something else!"

My smile is slightly strained, as I ask: "So how many would you like?"

Apparently nobody was ready to pay for the drinks, either, even though they were all ready to participate in their consumption. After several attempts to find out who might settle the bill, Engineer 1 finally says, "I can pay this, and Eero's and Heikki's drinks. Oh, and Sami's and Pentti's – they're sitting somewhere down the back!"

I: "Ok… but what are they having?"

Engineer 1: "I don't know! But I'd like to pay for them now."

On the next row "Pertsa" informs my junior colleague that he'll pay for "that guy in the red shirt on row 13, and the three guys in checkered shirts sitting in front of him, and the other 17 guys somewhere in the front."

At the back of the plane, my senior colleague had already served "the 17 guys sitting somewhere in the front", and was now desperately trying to find Pertsa in a striped shirt, who had promised to pay. We had 12 minutes of flight time left.

AS I WAS giving out newspapers from the newspaper trolley, a passenger asked me for a GT. I desperately hunted for a "Göteborgs Tidning", until I finally understood that he wanted a gin and tonic. The next day, as I was serving drinks, a passenger asked me for an FT. "What's in it?" I asked. "No, a newspaper. The Financial Times?"

THIS HAPPENED ON a flight from Shanghai to Helsinki soon after we started charging for spirits. The change had upset a lot of our passengers - Scandinavians in particular. The young flight attendant serving drinks had already been subjected to some, well, not very pretty language when she asked for five euros for a gin and tonic. The passenger returned the drink, and my colleague moved on to the next row. "So hard liquor costs now, does it?" asked the passenger on the next row. "Fine, then I'll just have a red wine and a beer, and tell you where you can shove your five-euro cognac!" My colleague handed him the drinks calmly, and replied, "I'm sorry, sir, there's no space. The previous row's gin and tonic is already up there." The passenger burst out laughing, and actually came to the rear galley later to buy a five-euro cognac.

"MUMMY, PASS THE ICE, PLEASE"

I WAS ONCE working on the same flight with my mother, a flight attendant as well. I noticed that the passengers were giving us funny looks as we served them, but I had no idea why. Once we got to the galley, my mother had a go at me. Apparently I had been repeating the word "mummy" throughout the service. "Mummy, pass the ice please, mummy, can I have some lemon, please, mummy, would you pass me a coke... Mummy, mummy, mummy!"

I WAS SERVING drinks, and had trouble hearing what an elderly Japanese gentleman was whispering, so I pushed my head a little closer, just as he was lifting his finger to point at the juice carton... His right index finger ended up in my left nostril.

There are quite a few parent-child teams working at Finnair, both in the cabin as well as the cockpit. At the beginning of the 1990s, on a flight to Beijing, the mother, who was about to retire, and her two daughters worked together in business class – a family affair. Occasionally you might come across a father as a captain and his son as the first officer on the same flight. We fly in two generations, offering experience and enthusiasm in the right proportion.

🥂 **FEMALE PASSENGER:** "WHAT kind of drinks do you have in there?"

I: "Juice, soft drinks, wine, beer, pretty much anything… What would you like?"

Female passenger: "I guess I'll have a glass of water, then."

🥂 **YEARS AGO, AFTER** several morning flights and yet another night of very little sleep, I found myself on a morning flight to London, working in its gargantuan business class. One unsuspecting man ended up being at the receiving end of my extreme clumsiness: I first hit him on the head with a coffee pot, and then dropped a large bottle of whisky in his lap. As I was collecting trash I nearly crushed his knee-cap, and later dropped an unopened can of coke on the same knee. I was starting to

worry at this point, but not nearly as much as that poor man. As I was setting up the sales trolley, I thought that I would have to try and ease the situation somehow. As I pushed the trolley on to the aisle, I shouted, "Be careful and save yourself, I am coming!" Everyone in business class burst out laughing. After all, the other passengers had seen what had happened, and probably wondered when they would get to be at the receiving end of such "hospitality". I gave the man a laundry voucher with an explanation as well, in case his wife would wonder why he smelt of whisky.

🥂 **ON A LEISURE** flight, the crew had a short lunch break between services. A passenger pushed aside the curtain and walked into the rear galley, and ordered some drinks with a loud voice. I said, "Just a minute sir," got up, wiped my moustache, cleared my throat and opened the door of a small cleaning cupboard and shouted inside, "Could I have two gin and tonics, a red wine and a beer, please!" The passenger seemed satisfied that someone "downstairs" was working on his order and returned to his seat.

"I'LL NOW READ OUT THE FLAVORS…"

WE USED TO serve fruit candies on very short flights. There were many flavors, and they were listed on our cabin information brief, in case a passenger would want to know. The problem was that nearly every passenger would ask what was what. The chief of cabin on my flight had apparently had enough of questions, as he announced, "Ladies and gentlemen, we are about to begin the inflight service, and we will be serving you some fruit candy. The flavors are as follows: yellow – orange, black – liquorice, purple – black currant…" He repeated the announcement once more, just to make sure everybody understood.

A PASSENGER WAS upset on a leisure flight as he had asked for a window seat, but had been given one on the aisle instead. The flight was full, and nobody in his immediate vicinity was willing to change seats. I wondered what I could do to cheer him up, and decided to make him a window. I took a trash frame and taped "curtains" from kitchen roll on it. I went up to the man and said, "I'm really sorry that our service chain has let you down today. However, to make up for your loss, I do have this portable window for you. Would you like me to hold it in place, while you eat your preordered vegetarian meal?" The passenger burst out laughing, and stayed in a good mood for the rest of the flight.

ON A FLIGHT from Madrid to Helsinki, I wanted to brush up on my Spanish, and tell the passengers in their own language what we were serving. The name of the dish is usually printed on the foil cover. So, every time I encountered a Spanish passenger, I placed my hand gently on the foil and said, "Este es horno", or (as I now know), "This is an oven". The passengers gave me strange looks, but I assumed they were in awe of my language skills, and so I carried on, smiling amiably.

A PASSENGER WAS dissatisfied with the vegetarian meal that he had pre-booked, but luckily he had brought something to eat along: a ham-and-cheese sandwich!

THERE WAS A well-known Finnish rally driver seated in business class on a European flight. My experienced and rather outspoken colleague decided to give him some motherly advice and said, "Young man, it's polite to take your cap off when you eat."

WE USED TO serve bacon and eggs in business class. A passenger once wanted to send his portion back to the pantry, so that I could fry the bacon some more. Mission impossible – we don't fry anything, as there are only ovens onboard.

ONE OF THE starter options in long-haul business class was smoked vendace. It wasn't a very popular choice that day, and in order to not run out of the other option, I decided to recommend the vendace, accompanied by ice-cold schnapps, to everyone. The passengers soon asked me for schnapps songs, which are a tradition in Scandinavian countries. So there I was, singing "Helan går" ("down in one") to the Swedes and "Nyt uitetaan muikku" ("dip the vendace") to the Finns. Everybody was happy.

A GROUP OF European school children were on their way to China, and entertained each other by constantly ringing the attendant call bells, which, at some point, we simply had to ignore. When we were serving the meals, a Swedish lady complained, "I've rung the call bell several times, but nobody has come. You announced that you're serving pasta with cheese sauce. Can you please make mine without the cheese?"

WE WERE DELAYED, and would land in Helsinki a few minutes late. As we were serving the meals, a passenger asked if he would be able to make his connecting flight (something that was impossible to predict at that point). My colleague offered, "If you eat really fast, you might."

A YOUNG WOMAN was going to Copenhagen, and complained, because Finnair didn't offer Fenno-vegan food as a special meal, that is, a meal that was prepared using only Finnish vegetables. I couldn't help wondering what she was planning to eat in Denmark.

A BUSINESS CLASS passenger once continuously praised the meal he was having. "This chicken is so delicious," he said. "What great chicken," he repeated. And again: "This chicken tastes marvelous."

I meant to say that I would "tell the chef", but somehow all that repetition got to me, and I ended up saying, "Thank you, sir. I'll tell the chicken."

 **A VERY SLIM** colleague of mine was clearing in passenger trays. A young man had moved his tray on to the next table, but had barely touched his meal, so she wasn't sure if he had finished. I suppose she was planning to say, "Have you finished?" or "May I take this away?" but accidentally uttered, "May I finish this?" The man was a little taken aback, but said, "Sure... go right ahead." My colleague realized that there was no good way to fix her blunder, so she just escaped the scene. A little while later, the same passenger was on his way to the toilet, and looked on with disbelief, as that same rake-thin flight attendant was eating baby food (puréed fruit) out of a jar. Well, it has been reported that with very little time to eat, flight attendants are often hungry onboard.

AN AMERICAN LADY was traveling in business class from Helsinki to St.Petersburg. The flight time is only approximately 30 minutes, which leaves us maybe 15 minutes to complete the service. The passenger was filling in her landing card with her meal tray in front of her. The safety belt sign was already on for landing, so I asked her, if I could take her tray. "Of course not, I haven't finished." I waited until the final approach announcement came from the cockpit and went back to her. "I'm really sorry, madam, but I have to take your tray now." "But I haven't finished!" she objected. "Well, madam, I do apologize that Helsinki and St. Petersburg are geographically situated so close to each other." She finally handed me the tray.

FEEDING THE 5,000

ON A FLIGHT from Aqaba to Helsinki a group of people had not been given any seat numbers, due to a system error at check-in. They consisted of couples, families with children, a nervous flyer, who didn't want to be separated from her friend, and many more. Miraculously we managed to find seats for them together, even the family of five. However, our troubles didn't end there, as we were short of passenger meals. We used crew meal trays and the contents of the crew snack box in order to have at least something to serve passengers on the last rows. We apologized and explained the situation to the passengers. As we collected the trays, the father of five (whose family initially wasn't seated together) asked, "Is it true that you gave your meals to us?" "Yes, we did," I answered with a smile. "You do your work with such compassion," he said, while pulling a book out from his seat pocket.

There was a picture of hands breaking break on the cover, which read, "Christ's Cookbook". It was the nicest thing a passenger has ever said to me.

WE USED TO serve cake in first class. Only one passenger wanted some, so I cut her a slice. Later in the galley, I noticed I had accidentally cut some cardboard with it. As I took her plate away, I asked how she liked the cake. "Very nice, she replied, but the bottom was a bit chewy."

I ONCE HAD a total blackout, and could not remember how to say "vadelma" (raspberry) in English. "This is soo delicious, this cake!" exclaimed an American passenger. "What berry is it?" "Um, it's… um…er…a famous Finnish berry…vadelm – yes, this is vadelm cake!" I stammered. "Vadelm? Hmm… I've never heard of vadelm before, but it's very nice."

ONCE, ON AN early morning flight to Oulu, I spilt coffee in a man's lap. Yup, you guessed it – right there. I apologized, and went to get a cloth to wipe with from the galley. I came back and began patting the man's trousers dry. Eventually, the passenger said, "Very good service, and I'd gladly let you continue, but you spilled coffee on the guy sitting in front of me." I wished the ground would have swallowed me.

THIS HAPPENED ON a flight from Helsinki to New York perhaps 15 years ago… We served cream cake for dessert. I was pleased to notice that all of the male passengers in business class appeared to be in good spirits. I didn't suspect anything out of the ordinary, though, until a man seated on the last row grinned and asked, "Is that on purpose, that Playboy bunny tail?" I took a look at my behind, which was sporting a huge dollop of cream. I must have accidentally brushed against the cake in the galley.

COFFEE IN THE BLUE POT, TEA IN THE BLACK

MY COLLEAGUE WAS pouring coffee, and I was following with a teapot. A passenger asked my colleague for tea. I suppose she meant to say, "Tea is coming right behind me," but instead uttered, "Tea

is coming from my behind," turned her back, and bent over to serve a passenger in the window seat on the other side…

I HAD A coffee pot in one hand, and tea in the other. "Would you like coffee or tea?" I asked a passenger. "No thank you, but what do you have in the other pot?" (What OTHER pot?) "Raspberry juice," I said, and moved on to the next row.

IF THE CABIN crew ask you whether you would like to have some coffee or tea, the correct answer in that situation is always, "Coffee, please" or "Tea, please". Not "guava juice", "A beer", "Vitamin B", "What do you have there?" or "Lactic acid tablets".

A CHARTER FLIGHT to Gothenburg was full of car salesmen. For some reason that we were not fully aware of, someone at Finnair had sold them a full leisure flight package: a beverage service, a hot meal service, and a sales and preorder service – with a flight time of one hour and 10 minutes. We barely had time to collect the trays before landing. Luckily, one of the men had a good eye for damsels in distress, and he decided to help out. He grabbed a black trash bag and ran with it through the cabin. The passengers emptied the contents of their trays in the bag, and stored the trays inside the seat pockets for landing. Once again, we just and just managed to complete the service! We were very grateful of the extra pair of hands, though.

Fish?   Beef?   Chicken?

I WAS WORKING on a leisure flight, when I spotted an actress that I greatly admire among the passengers. Sadly, her career was then on a downward spiral. "Any trash? Any trash?" I said as I pushed the trash trolley along the aisle. As I got to the actress she peeked inside the half-trolley and said, "I won't fit in there!"

WHY, OH WHY, do passengers insist on defying the laws of gravity when I walk along the aisle with a tray full of trash, and see if they can fit just one more cup on? They never can.

A MAN ONCE tried to fit an empty wine bottle on a full tray of trash. I opened my mouth to tell him that I would go and empty the tray and come right back, when he actually tried to put the bottle in my mouth…

WE WERE FLYING to Toronto at the time when Russians need-ed a special permit to travel abroad, and they could not do so very often. Smoking, however, had already been outlawed. I caught a tall and well-built Russian man leaning against the wall outside a lava-tory and smoking a cigarette. I'm about 5 ft 5 with high heels, yet I boldly approached him with a cup of water (intended for the cigarette), and said, "It's not allowed to smoke here. Please extinguish your ciga-rette." He smiled and blew smoke rings in my face. "Ya ni panimaju (I don't understand)," he replied. We both repeated our phrases a few times, but made no progress. A super-charismatic female purser, whom half the men feared, arrived on the scene. She held out her hand, and said, "Your passport, please." The man dumped his cigarette in the glass, pulled out his passport from his breast pocket, and began speaking fluent English. I'm pleased that I got to witness someone learn a lan-guage so rapidly!

"SUCH A NICE AFTERSHAVE"

I SUPPOSE SOME people are embarrassed to go to the toilet on board, let alone ask where it is, and will just try any door, no matter how narrow or oddly placed it is. On the Super Caravelle, a pas-senger apparently attempted to go and do his business outside, as he was heading straight for the entry door. I guess he didn't remember coming in through it.

THERE ARE SEVERAL different kinds of cupboards in various shapes and sizes on the Airbus. A Finnish politician decided that a small and narrow cupboard for crew bags must be the toilet, and was half-way inside before realizing his mistake.

THEN THERE ARE the passengers (usually male), who have no trouble finding the right door, but take a neatly folded newspaper along with them. One Englishman was very annoyed about the interruption, when I knocked on the door and asked if everything was ok. The next passenger in line had already waited 15 minutes for her turn.

ON A LEISURE flight, we suddenly heard a high-pitched voice from the toilet shouting, "I'm reeeeeaaaaadyyyyyyyy, come and wipe!" We didn't think that was included in our job description, so we made an announcement, "Ladies and gentlemen, if one of you has left a little boy in the toilet, he would like you to know that he's finished his business now. Thank you."

THERE WAS A little turbulence, and I was on my way to the rear galley, when I literally bumped into a small man, who was standing on an armrest and trying to open the overhead locker. I asked what the matter was, and if I could perhaps help in some way. The gentleman asked me to open the overhead locker and help him to get in, as he wasn't feeling well due to the bumpy weather, and he also needed to pee. I suggested he would be better off going to the toilet, and he replied angrily, "What do you think I'm trying to do, it's just so darn hard to get in!" I then realized that there was a sign for the lavatory on the locker, with an arrow pointing toward the rear (or up, I suppose, if you're really imaginative).

ON A LEISURE flight, I noticed that a couple, who had had more than a few drinks, was trying to get into the toilet together. Joining the mile high club would probably have taken them quite a while, and there was a long queue, so I said, "Could you complete your club application another time, please, just one at a time in the toilets!" They didn't seem too upset.

ONCE A GENTLEMAN came out of the rear toilet rubbing his chin, and said, "You have quite a nice after shave in there." The fragrance in question was the air freshener, of course.

"ONE OF THOSE WOMEN'S THINGS"

THE TOILET PAPER holder onboard aircraft is a small, white, plastic tube. Sometimes, if the roll is finished, the holder might come off and fall on the floor. I suppose that due to its shape and color people mistake it for a super-sized tampon, a word that they apparently find embarrassing to say out loud, as some of the terms I've heard used for the holder are:

"One of those women's things"

"You know…a thing."

"T-A-M and so on…"

"Come and see for yourself"

"A-hem…" (Passenger clears his throat and points at the floor).

THERE WAS A little boy on a flight from Malaga to Helsinki traveling as an unaccompanied minor, and apparently he was used to getting first class service wherever he went. He rang the call bell often, and had managed to fully employ everyone sitting around him. One was buttering his bread, the other cutting his steak into pieces, and the rest of us fulfilled any other requests. However, even royalty have to go to the toilet sometimes. The boy pressed the attendant call button in the toilet, and my colleague, a childless steward, went to check on the boy. "I'm done, you can come and wipe now!" If you're old enough to travel on your own, you're old enough to take care of your needs in that department, thought the steward, and handed the boy some extra-soft Kleenex and wet-wipes. After a while, the boy walked out of the toilet by himself. I sometimes wonder, if this was a story that the boy was later proud to recall? It probably wasn't, but definitely one that he would remember.

IN THE QUIET hours of the night, I was in the rear galley while most of the passengers were asleep. A young Japanese woman came out of the toilet, and came up to me with a quizzical look on her face. I asked if I could help her. "I have difficult shiit," she said. "I beg your pardon?" I asked, hoping that I had misheard her. "I have difficult shiit. I have window shiit and my husband is sleeping in the aisle shiit." I still wasn't sure how I could help her, but I was nevertheless relieved that she had a seating problem and not a pooping problem.

ON THE DC-9, the rear jumpseat was between two toilets facing each other. There was a long queue, and a man standing in it asked angrily, "How long will this still take?" I leaned forward, opened the lid of the ashtray that was on the door, and pretended to peek in. Then I opened the lid of the ashtray on the other door. I pointed to the left and said, "Oh, this will take a while yet, but the toilet on the right should vacate soon."

WE FOUND DENTURES in the toilet on a flight from Tokyo to Helsinki, and wondered how to find the owner… We considered announcing, "Ladies and gentlemen, could you please check that your teeth are in place, since we have found some extras. You can claim them in the rear galley." We decided that we needed to be more discreet, so we referred to the dentures as "personal belongings", and managed to find their rightful owner.

ON A LEISURE flight back in the 1980s, a drunken male passenger was throwing up in the rear toilet, and accidentally, his dentures fell into the toilet bowl. I watched in awe as a colleague pulled disposable gloves on and fished the passenger's dentures out. We barely had time to rinse them, when the man grabbed them, stuck them back in his mouth and sailed back to his seat.

"WAS IT ONLY THE UPPER ARCH, MADAM?"

"EXCUSE ME, BUT the missus lost her dentures while throwing up…" I took the sick bag, fished out the dentures, cleaned them and brought them back to the woman as discreetly as possible. "Was it only the upper arch, madam?" I whispered. She snapped them back on right then and there, and replied smiling widely, "Yes, dear, just the upper arch." Another time, a set of dentures had to be fished out of a trash bag, as a passenger had put them into her coffee cup and then handed her tray to the flight attendant. It seems that if you lose your dentures on a Finnair flight, you have a better than average chance of getting them back.

I WAS CHECKING the cabin for takeoff, when I noticed that a man sitting on a bulkhead row had removed his prosthetic leg, and was literally sitting with his leg in his lap. I had started flying quite recently, and could not think of a good way to ask the passenger if I could put his leg up in the overhead locker, or secure it with a seatbelt on to the next seat. I simply informed the chief of cabin about the situation and slipped back to my duty station at the back. I'm not entirely sure what she did about the matter.

I WAS SITTING on the rear jumpseat with a colleague after the meal service on a flight from Vaasa to Las Palmas, when an elderly male passenger came up to us and started to sing:

Your eyes shine their light on me
and bring me constant joy.
I believe in love at first sight
and therefore sing this song.

You are the best, and beautiful too
like a pretty doll you are
claiming the affection of men near and far.

Like a butterfly you flitter by
and I can't take my eyes off you.
Oh, how I wish to reach out and touch you
but I know I can't.

You are the best, and beautiful too...

I daydream and think of you
wondering if you think of me too.
I hope to see you again
as your happiness I would guarantee.

I have these words on a signed piece of paper, dated October 10, 2004. I just haven't had the heart to throw it away. A good thing too, as now the song will finally be published, as an ode to all flight attendants. Thank you sir, whoever you are.

ONCE, ON A flight to Delhi, I heard a business class passenger huffing and puffing in his seat, until he said to me, exasperated, "Please put this somewhere!" and handed me his prosthetic leg. I wish I could have seen my expression.

YEARS, AGO, WE had some cosmetics on offer in the business glass toilets, and Elizabeth Arden's Blue Grass hand lotion was among them. As I was pushing the inflight sales trolley along the aisle, a woman insisted on buying "that lovely hand cream you sell onboard". I apologized that we didn't have it for sale, and showed her the product selection. "I know that you sell it onboard," she insisted, "Every time my husband goes away on business he brings me some of that hand lotion from the aircraft!"

ANNOUNCEMENTS ARE A tricky business. I've accidentally told passengers in my sales PA that a bag we had for sale could take 30 euros, when I meant 30 kilos. A colleague recommended that very same bag by saying that it was made out of helicopter cloth, when he naturally meant parachute cloth. I've told customers that a product has a one day warranty, when I've meant one year...

I SOLD A Moomin box candy selection to a young girl, and asked if she'd like a bag for it. "Yes, please, so that I won't give in to temptation."

"DO YOU PUT THAT ON YOUR UNDERARMS?"

A PASSENGER ON a flight to Oslo was looking at a deodorant, and took a long time to decide whether to buy it. My male colleague asked, "Do you find it too expensive?" "No," the passenger replied smiling, "After all, we have oil in Norway." "Oh. Do you put that on your underarms then?" my colleague continued.

A MALE PASSENGER asked my colleague, who was a bit plump, if she knew of a good "wrinkle cream". The flight attendant handed him a chocolate bar, and said she used it herself – and didn't have a single wrinkle. The passenger laughed, and ended up buying a face cream as well as the chocolate.

IN THE OLD days, we had metal seals for the trolleys. We were about to land in a short while, and I had just put the sales trolley back in its place. As I snapped the seal closed, I noticed to my horror that the galley curtain was caught inside the trolley door. The purser saw it, and said, "Just cut it, I guess." I hesitated (but only for a second), and then cut the curtain with scissors. It was a bit tricky, but I managed to finish the job just as the purser came back. She laughed, and remarked, "I meant the seal."

WE WERE ON a flight to New York, and a small, slim, elderly American woman with good posture stretched and exercised throughout the eight-hour trip over the Atlantic. She was more flexible than young girls. When we got to JFK, the local handling agent said that he had the requested wheelchair waiting. We were a little confused, as we hadn't noticed anyone with reduced mobility onboard. Then our old ballerina came slowly and half-bent down the aisle. She said she needed assistance and had indeed requested someone to meet her with a wheelchair. As we were waiting in our own line at immigration, we noticed how she was taken past the long queues, and, of course, received assistance with her baggage as well. What a clever trick! I'll have to remember that when I retire.

ON A NIGHT flight from Bangkok to Helsinki, I was alone in the rear galley, when a woman asked, "I need to dance now; where can I dance?" I could hardly speak for my surprise, but pointed at the small space between the aisle and the rear toilet. She put her headphones on and danced a full set from can-can to twist. The purser was a bit taken aback as he came back to the galley.

ABOUT HALF-WAY TO China a woman came to the galley and asked for something. None of us could understand what she wanted. She grew increasingly frustrated as we offered her something to drink, eat, napkins, earplugs… Finally she just shrugged and walked away. A little while later, I saw her standing on her head, legs propped up against the toilet door. She had a pillow under her head. Ah, a pillow! That's what she had asked for, of course.

ON A LEISURE flight on April Fools Day, I decided to have a little fun, and announced, "Ladies and gentlemen, one of the passengers has lost his hamster. The little guy is small and brown, and his name is Button. Could you please check all your luggage, shoes, and loose items on the floor, but please be careful not to scare him away. Thank you." Everyone began rummaging in their bags for the poor lost hamster. In my "after landing" announcement, I wished everyone a nice and sunny holiday, and reminded them that it was the first of April.

ON A FLIGHT from Puerto Plata, as I was serving drinks a young man suddenly asked me what I did about sex after long flight. "I beg your pardon?" I asked, thinking I must have misheard him. "You see, my girlfriend is eagerly waiting for me at home as I've been gone for two weeks, and I really don't think I'll have the energy. I thought maybe you as flight crew have a solution to this kind of dilemma?"

WE WERE TAKING a group of World War II veterans on holiday. One of the elderly men was looking at my junior colleague and remarked, "If I could just get one like her by my side..." "Then what, exactly?" asked his friend. "You'd get a heart attack and that would be it!"

ON ONE OF my flights recently, all the topics of conversation among the crew appeared to stay below the waistline. At the end of the flight, as I went to take something into the cockpit, I had to say, "Guys, I'm sorry – I can't keep up anymore. They do say that women think about sex only once in every five minutes, and men every three minutes." "Come back in two minutes, then!" remarked the first officer.

ONE EARLY MORNING, we were returning from a layover in Vaasa. At the end of the flight, a male passenger told me that the zip of my skirt was undone. As I awkwardly thanked him, he said, "Oh, I would have told you already at the beginning of the flight, but then I thought you'd think I was staring at your behind!"

WHEN I HAD been flying for only a couple of weeks, a man suddenly asked me, "So, are you in the mile high club yet?" I had no idea what he was talking about, as I had never heard the term before. I thought he must have meant how many miles I'd flown by then, and tried to add up the flights that I'd done so far. "Now, I must admit I'm not quite sure, let me go and check with my senior colleague," I told the man, and went to ask my colleague if I was in the mile high club. Yes, you can imagine the look on the senior flight attendant's face - and the passenger's.

I WAS QUITE young and working in business class on my own. An ordinary-looking man was reading the tabloids. The lead story that day was the publication of the "Great Finnish sex survey". The man ordered a gin and tonic, and then asked me, "So, have you participated in this survey?" "No," I replied. "Have any of your friends?" he continued. "Not that I know of," I muttered, and went back to the galley where I stayed for the rest of the flight.

A SLIGHTLY TIPSY man stumbled into the rear galley on the MD-11, and after looking at my colleague for a while, remarked, "What a mare!" My colleague wasn't offended in the least, but retorted, "I see you know your horses." He admitted to owning several trotters, and was now on his way to watch a horse race in Shanghai.

A FINNISH MAN came into the galley just as I was crushing a plastic water bottle by stepping on it. "Yes, that's the way to crush even a thicker bottle – just put enough weight on it!" Ah, the Finnish compliment.

IN THE MIDDLE of the night, somewhere over Siberia, as I was talking with a passenger, he suddenly asked, "If you noticed someone peeking in from a window *right now*, would you tell anyone?" I still wonder to this day.

IN THE 1970S, an old man asked me how long I'd been flying. "Eight years," I replied. "What! And you still haven't found a husband?"

OUR DEPARTURE WAS delayed due to some technical problem, and three women had their knickers in a bit of a twist. "How do you not inform people beforehand about this kind of thing?"

"IT'S VERY DIFFICULT TO PLOUGH SNOW BEFOREHAND"

THE FLIGHT WAS full, a blizzard was raging outside, and the runway was open for maybe 20 minutes at a time, which caused major delays. One man demanded to know why we weren't prepared for this kind of thing in advance. "Sir, we do our best," I replied, "but you must understand how difficult it is to plough snow beforehand."

WE WERE ON a re-fueling stop in Gander, Canada, many years ago. It was a typical winter day, and we were all set to go, when an aircraft that was landing slid off the runway. The runway had to be closed, of course, and snow ploughed off another one, and all that took some time. I remember one passenger asking, "Why does Finnair use airports that are subjected to snow and ice?"

"WHY WASN'T THE de-icing done last night?" asked an angry passenger on a morning flight that was a few minutes delayed due to the de-icing of the aircraft. "Well, sir, you don't scrape your car windows the previous evening, do you?"

De-icing the aircraft means removing any snow and ice from its fuselage and wings.

OCCASIONALLY, YOU COME across these couples, who are such fine people that they don't speak to the hired help, or at least interaction is very limited. There was one such couple onboard, and the wife would not speak to me at all; the husband took care of all requests. Towards the end of the flight, the man called me over as the wife prompted, "Ask now. Go on, ask her!" The husband asked; "My wife is dying to know how your legs are so slim and toned, even though you're so fat?" I lifted my skirt a little and said, "Well, I'm glad she appreciates them."

THIS HAPPENED ALONG time ago, when no man would voluntarily shave his head. A bald man pointed at my colleague standing a little further away. "How can she be so fat?" he asked. "But doesn't she have lovely, thick hair?" I retorted.

 I REMEMBER THAT an American tourist once asked if Lapland was open that day.

 A FINNISH COLLEAGUE was talking to a Japanese group leader in Japanese. Two women were queuing for the toilet, and one of them pointed at the flight attendant and remarked to her friend, "Wouldn't have thought her to be Japanese. I would have said she's Finnish, if I didn't know better."

 A MIDDLE-AGED MAN once stopped me on the aisle and said, "I fly more than you do!" What should one say to that? I just smiled.

 A LITTLE GIRL was bawling her head off in her mother's lap. Nothing helped, until one of our legendary stewards pushed his round face close to the little girl's and said, "Don't cry, little Ines. Tomorrow we're going to the amusement park!" She stopped crying, and sat totally silent for the rest of the flight.

 I WAS WORKING on a flight from Düsseldorf to Helsinki. The passenger seated on the last row, a handsome young man, looked at me in the eyes and whispered, "Marry me!" I told the pilots that I was too busy to bring them their coffee, as I'd just received a proposal. He did ask some odd questions, but you can't be too picky when you get to my age! Just before landing I noticed he was carrying a white notebook with a Finnair logo, the same that had been given out to personnel a couple of years earlier. "Are you Finnair staff?" I asked him. "Not exactly," he replied, "I'm a Quality Hunter." I was a bit disappointed.

Quality Hunters are drawn from the public, and they travel on Finnair flights and make observations about the service, trying to come up with suggestions to improve it.

 ONE ROCKER WITH a bad reputation brought tears to our eyes. Why? For the way he treated his wife – like she was the most fragile and precious being. Once again, the younger generation knew better, as "that hooligan" turned out to be every mother's favorite son-in-law.

 HEAVY LIFTING IS left to stewards when possible, but not everyone agrees with this. I was trying to pull out a catering box that was high up, and the cable to pull it from was broken, so I couldn't reach. I asked my taller male colleague if he could lend me a hand. He replied, "Same job, same pay," and walked off. I stood dumb-struck, and in 25 years of flying, haven't thought of a snarky comment to match, should the situation repeat itself.

 A COLUMBIAN MAN was on the Helsinki-Oulu-Rovaniemi flight. I had studied Spanish at Guadalajara University in Mexico, and was perhaps a little over-enthusiastic to speak it any time I had the chance. We were talking about everything from cooking to politics, and every now and then I would excuse myself and go and do some work. We landed, passengers left, and new ones entered. We were just about to land in Rovaniemi, when the man asked me, "When will we arrive in Oulu?" Oh dear. Luckily for me, he was a typical Latino, who just laughed it off, and said, "Oh well, at least I get to see a bit of Finland." I don't know how they got him from Rovaniemi to Oulu, and was too embarrassed to ever ask the company. I started going to conversational Spanish classes after that, so that no passenger would have to suffer from my willingness to practice my language skills again.

"THAT'S A WHOLE OTHER COUNTRY, ISN'T IT?"

 THIS HAPPENED AT Charles de Gaulle Airport in Paris, which is somewhat notorious for losing luggage, and occasionally passengers. We had to do a headcount before departure, and I just could not get the number of passengers onboard to match the figure at the gate. I counted altogether three or four times, and always seemed to have one passenger too many. Finally the ground agent (in a hurry to get us to leave) muttered something about an infant not having been in their figure, and we were good to go. As I was checking the cabin for takeoff, an American woman grabbed my arm and asked, "Excuse me, but did you say this flight is going to Helsinki?" "Yes, I did," I replied. "That's where we're headed." The passenger pulled out her boarding pass and said, "But I have an SAS flight to Stockholm!" I called the cockpit immediately, but with onward connections from Helsinki, and the flight already slightly delayed, the captain decided not to turn back. "Tell her that in spite of what it says on her boarding pass, she now has a Finnair flight to Helsinki!" I relayed the information to the passenger, who exclaimed, "Oh dear, that's a whole other country, isn't it?" What could I do but agree. The connections from Helsinki to Stockholm are quite good, and our stow-away got to her final destination later on the same day.

SOMETIME IN THE mid 1990s, three Austrian men were on their way to Tampa (TPA), Florida. They had to fly to Helsinki first, which they found a bit strange, but didn't mind too much, considering the tickets had been so cheap. At the departure gate of the flight to Tampere (TMP), they began wondering if the aircraft, a 42-seater propeller plane parked at the gate, could make it across the Atlantic Ocean. They had bought tickets to the wrong city.

THE PILOTS HAD to abort our landing to Helsinki-Vantaa at a very low altitude. As a reason for the disruption, the captain announced, "There was a wild animal on the runway." We later found out that the animal in question was a rabbit.

HERE'S A SADDER story. We were returning from a holiday destination. There was a man onboard who appeared very ill. His wife and children were with him. We had some empty seats that day, so I arranged for the man to be able to lie down. The children behaved as children do, they played among themselves and went to talk to their father every now and then. The mother looked drawn and serious. The father was very weak and appeared to be in pain; but he was still very friendly and positive. We talked a little on the flight, and they told me that they were on a last family holiday, before it was time for the father to leave them. As an emotional person and a mother myself, I was deeply touched by this. Some time later, I noticed the father's obituary in the newspaper, and it made me very sad.

🥂 **I WAS WORKING** on the last flight of the day to Vaasa. A little old lady walked in and asked me if this was the flight to Vaasa. "Yes, definitely," I replied. Well, I should have guessed it! The weather was so bad in Vaasa that after two attempts to land, the captain opted for the closest airport, and we landed in Kokkola. The little old lady was extremely upset, because had she not specifically checked with me that the flight would go to Vaasa! I tried to explain about weather conditions and flight safety, but I don't think she really grasped what I was trying to say. On her way out, she hissed, "You really don't know anything about anything, do you? And the pilots flew so badly as well, it was a terribly bumpy flight!"

CHAPTER 7

SPEAKING GIBBERISH

THE LANGUAGE OF aviation is English, but as most of us at Finnair are native speakers of Finnish, words that are pronounced in a similar way can sometimes confuse us, for example, the rather unfortunate pair *flight time* and *lifetime*… Lack of sleep can hamper our ability speak, or understand, any language – even our own – which causes some amusing situations too.

CREW STORIES

I WAS WORKING in business class on a flight from Shanghai to Helsinki, and the lunch options were duck breast and beef noodles. I had slept badly the night before, and was getting a little tired. I picked up the bread basket and offered, "Would you like some breast?" The man laughed and replied, "Maybe I'll just take a bread roll this time. Thank you for the offer, anyway." I wish I would have had an ejection seat.

SINCE 1995, FINNAIR has collaborated with UNICEF in a fundraiser called "Change for Good." Or "Change for God", as one purser announced.

KAR-AIR OPERATED ITS first official ATR-72 flight to Lappeenranta. There were mainly company executives and media representatives onboard. On the ATR, the chief of cabin worked at the rear part of the aircraft, "behind the scenes", one could say. The Deputy Head Stewardess at the time liked attention, so on the return flight she suggested, "You work at the back, and I'll stand there in front and smile." Fine by me, and indeed, everything went fine until it was time for me to announce in English, and I said, "Our estimated lifetime is 25 minutes."

WE ANNOUNCE ANY code share partners in the "Welcome onboard" announcement. On a flight from Stockholm I was announcing by heart, "Finnair is operating this flight as a joint service with…absolutely nobody but itself. Have a nice flight!"

A SWEDISH WOMAN on a flight to Bromma asked for some water. I meant to ask "Still or sparkling?" but got a little confused with my terms and asked, "With or without gas?" She started laughing and replied, "Oh, without gas I hope."

"I LOVE YOU ALL"

THE FIRST OFFICER was a recent graduate, and his announcements were still a bit shaky He had meant to begin, "I would like to welcome all of you onboard… and end with, "I wish you all a very pleasant flight!" I suppose there was an interruption from the air traffic control or something, as all he managed to say was, "I love you all… Thank you."

JUST BEFORE LANDING, the cockpit would announce "final approach". This procedure was not in use for very long, as I suppose it sounded a bit too final in passengers' ears.

I WAS WORKING for the fifth evening in a row. Every day had consisted of at least four individual flights. I was the chief of cabin, and we had just landed from Stockholm to Helsinki. "Ladies and gentlemen, welcome to Kuopio…I mean Stockholm. No, I mean Helsinki, of course. It is now twenty past four…I mean, twenty past six… Thank you for flying Finnair, have a nice weekend!" It was Tuesday. "I hope you get to go home now," said a man on the first row.

ON A FLIGHT to Rome, my colleague was excited for the opportunity to practice her Italian, which had become a bit rusty. She talked to a passenger who worked for Alitalia. She was going to Rome on holiday soon; could the man maybe recommend a nice hotel, "un albero per noi?" Giovanni replied with a laugh, "Ci sono molti alberi in centro di Roma." *Albero* means tree, and *albergo* hotel.

I WAS HANDING out blankets in business class. I got to a Swedish passenger and drew a blank. "Vill ni har en blanket?" I attempted. The man looked at me like I was a half-wit, for holding out a blanket but offering him a form.

THERE WAS A big group of Spanish customers and I wanted to announce in Spanish, but couldn't find the right papers. "Close enough," I thought, and grabbed the announcements in French, and began, " El comandante X con su *equipaje* les desea bienvenidos…" That means, "The captain and his baggage would like to welcome you onboard…"

I WAS THE chief of cabin on a domestic flight. Our work day had begun early in the morning, and we were now on a triangular flight Helsinki-Oulu-Rovaniemi-Helsinki. I accidentally announced that we were going to Rovaniemi, and somehow changed the captain's last name from Virtanen to Ahonen. Passengers to Oulu were alarmed, of course, so a colleague came to ask me to repeat the announcement and to say that we were going to Oulu as well, and that the cap-

tain's name was Virtanen. I began again, but once I started announcing in Swedish, I again said Rovaniemi and Captain Ahonen. "Would you please try and remember for the duration of the entire announcement that we're going to Oulu as well, and that the captain is Virtanen?" whispered my colleague again. Third time's the charm, and finally in English, I managed to get it right.

I WAS WORKING in business class on a flight to New York, and there were two particularly nice men sitting on the first row. I had served them throughout dinner, and as they were settling down to rest, I said, "If you have any other desires you would like me to fulfill, just let me know." I knew it didn't quite come out right the moment I said it, so I added, "As long as they are decent ones." One of the men burst out laughing, but the other had failed to hear me. "What did she say?" he asked his friend. "Please don't ever tell," I pleaded. "I won't," replied the man, "Nobody would believe me anyway."

NO WONDER MY daughter wrote her Ph.D. dissertation on circadian rhythm disorders and their connection to an individual's general health, as she had to watch and listen to me throughout her childhood. I remember how I once asked her to look for a lost button, which was black but silver-colored, and even though she repeatedly asked me what color the button was, I kept repeating, "A black button, which is silver." I think I'd just come back from New York or something.

IRON BIRD

The heavy iron bird flew
with sleeping chicks inside her belly.
She flew east, she flew west
engines roaring as she journeyed
through the night.

The heavy iron bird flew
drawing a white line in the sky
searched for a place, then another
yet a third
to let the young ones out of the nest.

The heavy iron bird flew,
grew wings from her body
then bounced on her belly,
seeped out the seeds,
chucked out the chicks.

Up flew the heavy iron bird
curving and turning as she climbed,
with new nestlings inside
on her usual path,
her restless rambles.

Sirpa Kivilaakso

CHAPTER 8

LANDING

TOWARDS THE END of the flight, the cockpit crew usually makes an announcement about the time of arrival and weather conditions at the destination. The cabin crew get a chance to sit down during landing, though even this time is not really rest, as we silently review what to do in case of an emergency. The passengers remain alert too, as they can usually watch the landing from their personal screens. On landing to Vienna, a man was upset because in his opinion, the aircraft did not stay in its lane. Emotions are heightened towards the end of a flight. A nervous flier will let out a sigh of relief; a business traveler feels like he is nearly home, and someone will ask shyly, if they can peek into the cockpit before leaving. Not everyone is happy, however. "Finnair never stays on schedule," grumbled a passenger, when a flight landed in Bangkok 30 minutes ahead of the scheduled time of arrival. "Finnair can no longer be trusted," complained another, on leaving the plane. "What is the problem?" I asked. "The captain is a woman!" continued the man. Passengers do often wonder about crew composition, which is usually random. On a flight with only stewards working, passengers thanked for a nice flight, but wondered why all the women had

MY BED

Luxurious sleep
at Grand Stanford Hong Kong
as opposed to
my Nordic dreams, plain and simple.
I need cushioning
more than ever.

Riitta Kiiveri

been left behind. Another once asked if Finnair rosters cabin crew by their hair color, since that day, we were all blonde.

Sometimes passengers don't say anything when they leave. Once, a rather drunken woman disembarked with a familiar-looking bag over her shoulder. She had accidentally mistaken the demo bag (containing equipment for the manual safety demonstration) for her own handbag. Some people like to make an impact as they leave, for example, one singer from the 1990s, who kissed a flight attendant right on the mouth as a means of thanking her for the flight.

"I'D RATHER TAKE A TAXI!"

If we park at a remote stand at Helsinki-Vantaa, the passengers are taken by bus to the terminal building. I stood at the rear door saying goodbye, when I noticed a passenger wondering around in the midst of catering trucks and baggage carts. I ran after him in order to get him on the bus. "I'd rather take a taxi!" he announced.

Stewards often make jokes about everything, but there are situations when even they are at a loss for words. One of those situations occurred, when a passenger asked a steward if he had ever considered working as a Santa Claus. "Give me a call, since you speak so many languages and look like Santa," said the man. The steward took a look at the man's business card, and indeed, he was from Rovaniemi (Santa's hometown), and the CEO of a company providing Santas for various international events.

A stewardess, however, declined the contact information of a male passenger at the door, and only later remembered that he had lost something and wanted to give her his information to pass on to the lost-and-found. He wasn't trying to pick her up!

A flight attendant will keep up appearances to the very last, and won't stop smiling even when facing a rather long way home. A colleague announced, "Ladies and gentlemen, we are going to park in outer space, so you have

bus transportation to the terminal building." I suppose she couldn't remember the correct term. As she realized her mistake, she nearly choked on her laughter, with the loudspeaker still on.

After the passengers are gone, the exhaustion sets in. The border control officers are sometimes surprised by a flight attendant, who will attempt to show her cell phone instead of her passport at the check-point. Her colleagues understand and know from experience, however, why she would knock on the door of her dressing room locker before opening it.

Understanding, and a lot of laughter, will follow an attempt to leave the dressing room without any trousers. Finding the car from the park-ing lot can be a challenge. A few have been about to call the police before remembering that they had got a lift to work, and sometimes, the police are actually needed. A policeman once helped a colleague break into her car, as she had started the car, loaded her bags in, and locked the door with the keys in the ignition.

Empathy and creativity are requirements for flight attendants. Or what do you say about a flight attendant, who took a passenger home, so that she wouldn't have to sleep at the airport? The flight was delayed, and there was a passenger seated on the last row, who, most likely, would miss her connecting flight to Oulu, and would have to wait for the next flight, which wasn't until morning. The flight attendant decided to help. She asked the passenger to collect her bags and meet her in the arrival hall, and took her to her house for the night. "I got there and my husband looked quite surprised. I didn't really get into it in much detail; I just told him that she was a passenger, who had lost her connection and would be staying the night." Her husband needed a minute to take it in, but then welcomed the passenger heartily. The passenger called her husband, and told him that she was spending the night at a flight attendant's house in Tikkurila, and would be home in the morning. The flight attendant didn't hear her guest leave in the morning, but found her business card on a counter in the hallway, with an invitation to come to Oulu at any time. The flight attendant's daughters sitting at the breakfast table must have thought she dreamt the whole thing.

CHAPTER 9

OUR INTERNATIONAL PASSENGERS

FINNAIR FLIGHTS ARE full of very different kinds of passengers. We take Finns to beaches, ski slopes and on city holidays. Asians come to Europe on our flights, and Europeans to Asia. We are lucky to be able to get acquainted with so many different countries, cultures and people while working. These encounters are often brief but memorable. Customer satisfaction is very important to us. If a passenger thanks us warmly at the door, we remember it for a long time. If we disappoint someone, we remember that even longer. People are the best and the worst variable in our work.

The higher the number of Asian passengers on Finnair flights, the more challenges we meet in making our customers happy. It is polite to use two hands to hand out beverages and food in Japan. Questions should not be formed in such a way that the Japanese would have to answer yes or now. Even small gestures are significant to the Japanese. Waving a hand in front of the face means "no" or "I don't know". The Chinese have trouble with horizontal communication, in which individuals are attempting to solve problems without a clear leader or authority figure. This is where cultures collide on flights. Finnish flight attendants like using their own initiative and take responsibility, whereas a Chinese passenger might want to speak with the purser right away. Chinese people smile a lot, and they have a good sense of humor. However, they can appear somber just as well, and that makes us think that they are unhappy with the service. Fortunately, we have local colleagues to help us out, and they sometimes say that we tend to wrongly interpret the lack of language skills as hostility.

"I'LL TRY" IS ALWAYS A GOOD ANSWER

The Koreans are very outspoken, which is rare in Asia. Aggressiveness among a wide range of other emotions might be used in order to convince someone. After getting acquainted with the happy Chinese and reserved Japanese, we had a bit of a shock when Finnair started flights to Korea in 2008. We poured a few coffees in the laps of Korean passengers too, before we learnt that they might just pull their cups away, without saying a word, when they've had enough. We recognized something familiar too; smiling too much might appear insincere, in both Finland as well as Korea.

You can't really say no to Indians either, and "I'll try" is then a handy solution for many situations. If the Japanese hand wave means "no" or "I don't know", in India, it could also mean "Go away". You should also refrain from touching an Indian, and this can sometimes cause misunderstandings, as Finnish flight attendants would gladly offer a helping hand to the elderly, or stroke a child's head.

Cultural differences are smallest among Europeans, but national traits still exist, and will manifest themselves on flights. Italians and Spaniards stand on the aisle talking to each other throughout the flight. The Swedes love peanuts. Norwegians always say "Ha det bra" ("take care") as they leave. The Germans often ask for a vegetarian option instead of the offered meal, and drink a lot of tomato juice. Fortunately, European hand gestures are fairly similar, so you won't make a terrible blunder if you need to resort to "sign language".

Coffee is a sacred cow for Finns. Our coffee is praised on flights back to Finland, and passengers usually drink several cups of it. In fact, if a coffee pot is not immediately within their line of vision, Finns will ask

TO CAIRO AND BACK

The best trip of my life
was to the city of Cairo.
I was carried by a majestic bird
in the care of friendly crew.

I saw the pyramids and tombs
that pharaohs left behind.
Looking back on all that I saw
my head spins in awe.

I've seen wonders of the world
and now I'm homeward bound
to treasure my memories
inside covers of gold.

I can't repay
the kindness of the crew
I can only express my gratitude
with roses in bloom.

Lauri Saari
(Written in Bulgarian air space
on march 22, 1989)

for it. These days, Finns are increasingly daring tourists. They often travel in small groups or even alone, without tour guides or group leaders. Finnish unaccompanied minors are usually bold and experienced flyers too. Finns feel quite patriotic about Finnair, and for many, air travel is associated only with Finnair's blue-and-white wings.

CHAPTER 10

SPECIAL SITUATIONS

MANY UNPLEASANT EVENTS that have occurred in the past few years have changed instructions, procedures and regulations in civil aviation either temporarily or permanently.

Finnair lost a steward in a hotel fire in Cairo, Egypt, in the 1990s, and since then, Finnair flight attendants have been very safety-conscious hotel customers. Every flight attendant must be aware of the nearest exits, and keep their room key and flashlight by the bed. Some flight attendants carry portable fire alarms, and I know one crew member who used to keep a smoke hood with her on work trips. An experienced pilot once advised a young flight attendant on what words to use in an emergency. If someone attacks you in the hotel, it's best to shout "Fire, fire!" as people will then come out of their rooms. If you scream "Help!" you might not get any assistance at all.

The BSE scare in Britain affected flights. In addition to asking where we got the beef that was being served, passengers kept a close eye on yoghurt and candy additives. For a while, passengers coming from the United Kingdom had to step into a pool of disinfectant after disembarking. That's all well and good, but what about the several pairs of possibly contaminated shoes that they might have carried in their suitcases?

The anthrax letters in the U.S. had an effect on safety regulations too. Flight crews are no longer allowed to carry any passenger mail, not even drop a postcard in the mailbox for them.

FACE MASKS AND DISPOSABLE GLOVES

The respiratory disease SARS caused a lot of fear and confusion in 2002-2003. The Ministry of Foreign Affairs in Finland issued guidelines for passengers traveling to Asia. Flight crews were given special instructions as well, and procedures for handling a suspected case of a contagious disease on flights were revised. During the SARS epidemic, cabin crew were allowed, and even urged for a while, to use face masks on flights. Unfortunately, the masks were not very comfortable or practical. Disposable gloves, however, came to stay. Collecting trash with gloves on is more hygienic for both crew and passengers.

The terror attacks on September 11, 2001 in New York nearly paralyzed the whole world for a while. Civil aviation was changed forever. Regulations at security control were tightened, as it was now a possibility that someone could use an aircraft as a weapon, or carry a bomb, with no regard to their own fate. Children were no longer allowed to visit the cockpit, which was a shame, as these visits had been fun for both the visitors and the pilots. Fortified cockpit doors came to stay. Tense, half-dressed passengers with plastic bags on their feet, standing in line at security control are a common sight at airports today. They place their belts, liquid bags, iPhones, pads and pods on plastic trays and pass through metal-detectors, are subjected to somewhat invasive pat-downs, and eventually get to run to the departure gate. The atmosphere at airports used to be more pleasant in the past. 9/11 will never be forgotten.

A flight attendant was watching the live broadcast from New York. Could this really be happening? In addition to the initial shock, other questions began to emerge. Where are our crew right now, and what must they be thinking? What are their families thinking? The Finnair crew members in New York at the time were safe, and the flight from Helsinki heading to New York turned back. The magnitude of the events did not reveal itself until later. It took about a week for the crew that was in New York to get back home.

BREAKFAST IN NEW YORK

I'd like to see Guernica,
  I think
in the morning at the Millennium.
  At Tiffany's,
a coffee
and a plastic omelet
  accompanied by a jackhammer.

At MoMA
  only a white wall
  and a sign:
        Guernica Paris 1937
                Picasso

Since the robbery,
  it's only imaginary...

Sirpa Kivilaakso

TIGHTENED SECURITY

A man failed in his efforts to detonate the explosives in his shoes on an American Airlines flight from Paris to Miami in December, 2001, just three months after 9/11. Since that close call, regulations regarding the transportation of liquids onboard aircraft were tightened. I am sure we've all forgotten to put our toothpaste or deodorant in a transparent bag at one time or another, but having to leave behind an expensive face cream, an oversized bottle of perfume, or cognac bought as a souvenir will sting a lot more.

The H1N1 pandemic from 2009 brought back procedures similar to the SARS era. Finns queued up for vaccinations, and business travelers carried Tamiflu in their hand baggage. Special health forms had to be filled in prior to entry to some countries, and body temperature was measured at Beijing Airport from both passengers and crew. We would stand in line and worry that normal post-flight exhaustion or a regular flu coming on might cause an elevated temperature. Our fate in such a situation would have been to wait on mattresses in quarantine for the fever to go down...

The volcanic ash cloud in 2010 caught the whole world by surprise, and brought air traffic in Europe on its knees. The problem was that nobody knew how long the conditions might persist – days? Weeks? Years? What amount of volcanic ash particles would be safe for flying? We survived even this setback, and managed to bring our passengers and crew home – some with quite a detour. A colleague, who was stuck in China, considered returning on the Trans-Siberian Express, in order to get home on time for May Day celebrations. They were stuck for eight days in total, watching news on CNN of deserted runways and chaotic terminal buildings, with people sleeping on the floors. It was a truly unique situation in the history of civil aviation. The sound of passenger jets had died down.

CREW STORIES

THE GULF WAR in 1991 culminated in Operation Desert Storm, when the U.S. jumped in from the sidelines. This war was the first "televised war", meaning that we saw a lot of events on live TV. I remember being on a flight to New York at the beginning of February, with very few passengers on the flight. Manhattan was a ghost town, as the U.S. was expecting retaliation, aimed at New York in particular.

AT EVERY CROSSROAD
FOLLOW YOUR
DREAM!
IT IS COURAGEOUS TO
LET YOUR HEART LEAD
THE WAY

ON SEPTEMBER 11, 2001 I was leaving for Tokyo, and just before boarding, we heard from the catering crew that a small plane had dived into a skyscraper in New York. The passengers knew a little more than we did, but we didn't really find out exactly what had happened until we got to Tokyo. The pilots received some information during the flight, but chose wisely to keep most of it to themselves. On October 9, I was back in New York, and visited Ground Zero with the rest of the crew. Most of the destruction was hidden from the public eye. It suddenly seemed absurd that people were queuing up with their cameras to catch a glimpse of the site from a small hole. We chose not to, and walked on.

IN BEIJING ON November 1, 2009, we saw at breakfast how it had started snowing, and wondered if we would be able to depart on time. Snow was very unusual in Beijing. We got to the airport, boarded the passengers, and taxied towards the runway. Then we taxied some more. We taxied and waited for our turn to take off for altogether six hours. Several aircraft appeared to give up, and turned back. When we finally got home, our total duty time was 16 hours and 20 minutes. I later heard a rumor that the Beijing Weather Modification Office would have artificially created the snowstorm in order to alleviate droughts.

IT WAS SPRING during the SARS epidemic, and the crew wore facemasks. A passenger made a comment about them, "I guess there's no need to smile now that you have those masks on." A steward on the flight borrowed my lipstick, and painted a smile on every mask. The passengers were pleased.

ON ANOTHER FLIGHT during the epidemic, a male passenger asked, "Since you've hidden your face, could you open a couple of buttons from your blouse?" My colleague, who was nearly 60, replied, "I don't think you'd enjoy the view that much, and it's probably better that my face is hidden too."

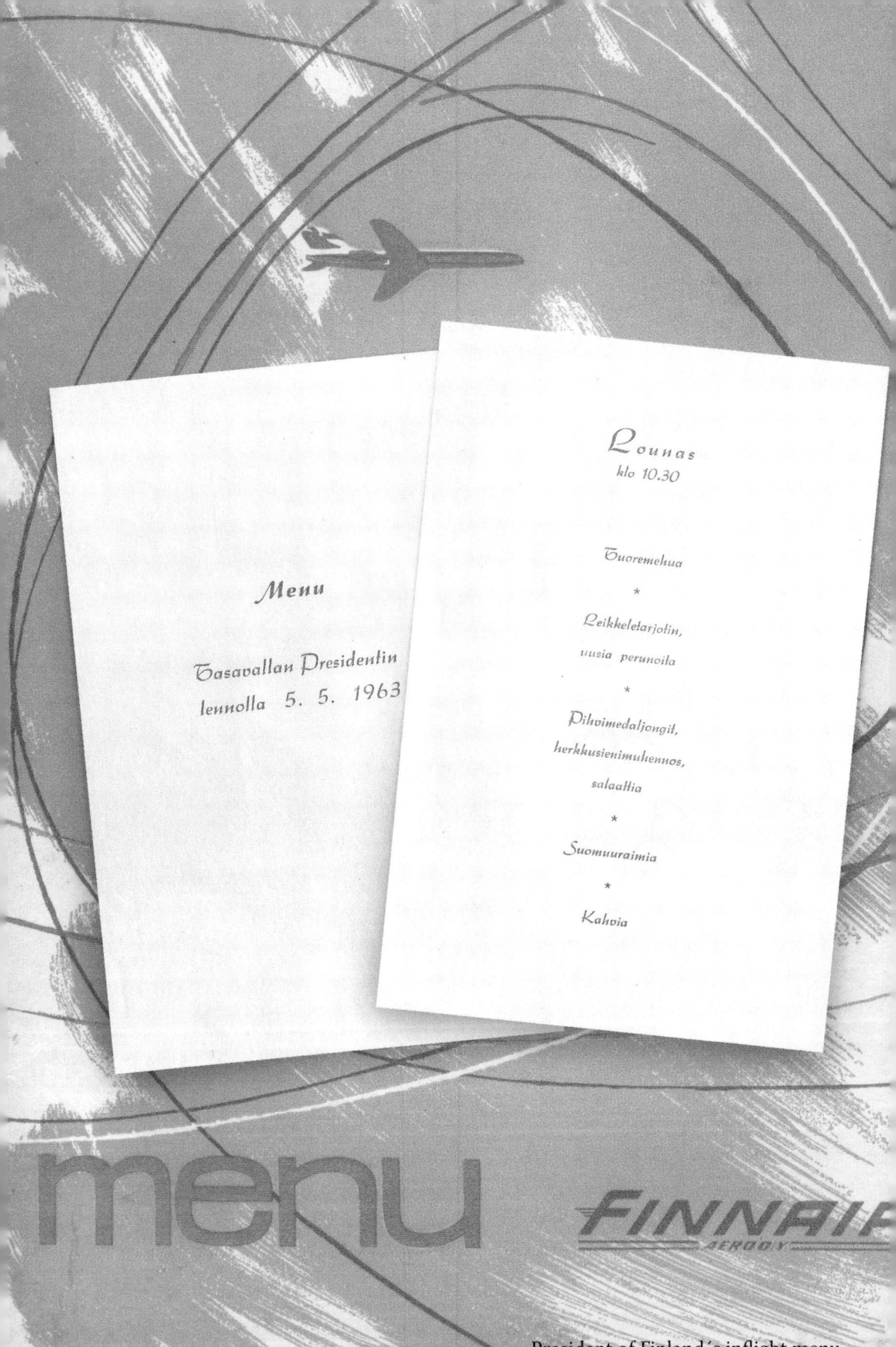

Menu

Tasavallan Presidentin
lennolla 5. 5. 1963

Lounas
klo 10.30

Tuoremehua

*

Leikkeletarjotin,
uusia perunoita

*

Pihvimedaljongit,
herkkusienimuhennos,
salaattia

*

Suomuuraimia

*

Kahvia

menu

FINNAIR
AERO O.Y

President of Finland´s inflight menu

CHAPTER 11

VERY IMPORTANT FLIGHTS

STATE VISITS, ROCK stars on tour, special charters, and celebrity passengers add their own flavor to our profession. Special flights require special preparation, and we do our best to make our guests feel welcome. In the case of state visits, the menus and service are planned in collaboration with different departments, and in great detail. Cabin crew are advised on how to address the passengers, and briefed on protocol.

Occasionally, a special charter might be an evacuation flight carrying Finnish citizens out of harm's way. Many Finns, and Finnair cabin crew have a lot of painful memories from flights to Helsinki from areas affected by the tsunami in 2004. Finnair brought back over 2,000 people within a period of five days 28.12.2004 – 1.1.2005.

Finnair flights have been the backdrop of the Brazil soccer and Finnish ice-hockey teams' World Championship celebrations. Many Olympic medalists have traveled on Finnair flights, and created a buzz among the crew.

This moment takes me away
From myself.
I flew far.
Watched like a bird
from high up and saw
everything getting smaller
and quiet down.
Far in the softness of space
in the light that
only exists here,
far away.
This memorable moment.
Everything was silent,
like the tinkle of dreams
in the early hours.
The power of love and goodness
was so vast
that it was no longer just in me.
It was all around me.
I think that for a moment
I had touched
Divinity.

Kati Kaivanto

CREW STORIES

PRESIDENT KEKKONEN WAS on a state visit to the United States. We served crab on the return flight. The aircraft was a DC-8, and the president and his entourage sat in first class, in a section that was isolated from the rest of the cabin. President Kekkonen preferred to be quite informal with the flight attendants. Before settling down to sleep, he asked me if I would sit by him and sing him a lullaby. I was quite shy and embarrassed for having been put on the spot. The president immediately noticed this, kissed my hand politely, and thanked for the lovely dinner, saying he would go and get some rest now. I was relieved, and impressed by his considerate and polite manner. Just before our arrival to Helsinki, the president went to the tiny toilet on the DC-8 to freshen up. When he came out, he looked like the flight had not been strenuous at all.

THE BELGIAN KING and queen were on an official state visit to Finland. The flights were operated with Finnair's Convair, and the crew was the same both ways. We received medals from the royal couple for our efforts. Protocol was tight; the captain wore white gloves and greeted the royal couple at the bottom of the aircraft steps. There was a red carpet, of course, and a band. The first officer stayed in the cockpit. During the flight, he expressed the need to go to the toilet, but was too embarrassed to walk by these important passengers. We brought him some empty soda bottles so that he could relieve himself.

IN 1963, IN Belgrade, the red carpet had been spread in front of the Caravelle steps, the band was playing and Josip Tito waiting to greet our president. The aircraft was to park by the steps, but slightly missed the mark. President Kekkonen was just about to step out, when the steps were adjusted. Seeing that the president was in danger, I grabbed him by his sleeve, which is against protocol. The president was angry, but calmed down rapidly, as we explained what had happened.

 THE FIRST LADY only drank sour milk on flights, and we had special glass pitchers for that. President Kekkonen gestured to his wife and remarked, "I can have doubles then."

"BETTER ON THE GROUND THAN..."

 THERE IS A biblical proverb in Finnish, "Better on the ground than in the mouth of the godless". I was unfortunate enough to blurt this out after accidentally dropping some petit fours, which were intended for the president, on the floor...

 I USED TO work at the information service at the airport, and in those days people would call and ask anything and everything under the sun. I once picked up the phone as a famous opera diva called – she was coming to Finland on her tour, and had some special requests. She wanted a red carpet, flowers, and expressed a wish that there would be no ex-beauty queens as cabin crew on her flight.

THE ROLLING STONES were once on a flight from Helsinki to Stockholm. The band members couldn't care less about the service, as they were busy amusing themselves by climbing over seat-backs and just lying about. Usually the last two rows on the Convair were not in passenger use, unless the flight was full. The Stones want-ed to sit on these very seats for landing, and also refused to fasten their seatbelts. I had to tell the captain that the cabin was not ready for land-ing, since some of the passengers would not buckle up. The captain said he would teach them a little lesson, and asked us to hold on tight. We approached normally, but then the captain suddenly pulled the aircraft up at a steep angle. After that, the flight engineer came out of the cock-pit to give the band a few murderous looks, after which they sat down in their own seats and fastened their seatbelts. A lesson well learned!

CHAPTER 12

ALL AROUND THE WORLD

FLIGHT CREWS SPEND up to a third of their nights per annum at hotels in various corners of the world. Packing is routine, and waking up in an Asian metropolis nothing out of the ordinary. When you travel a lot, you become a creature of habit. A work trip is not the same as a leisure trip, but a part of our normal daily lives. Someone might do all their grocery shopping in Düsseldorf, another buy her children's toys in New York. A third might spend the extra time on a layover studying for an exam, and a fourth use the available time for exercising. Routines bring security; it feels good to eat at your favorite restaurant, or walk down a familiar street. Not all destinations are as attractive, of course. When you know that you have trouble sleeping in Korea, you don't really look forward to going there. In addition, you might have to leave a sick child at home, or stop an argument unresolved. Joys and sorrows follow you around the world – hearing that your child got a good grade on her math exam is just as important heard at the hotel pool in Bangkok as it would be at the dinner table at home.

Even though flight attendants are experienced travelers, we still meet with surprises, particularly when our tired and jetlagged brains play tricks on us. Asian cultures and communities are different from our own; toilet seats in Japan seem to have a life of their own. They have many different functions, and the seat itself is heated. If the warmth of the seat isn't enough to startle you, you will be worried by the time you need to flush. I once waited in a shopping mall for a colleague to come out of the ladies room. She had mistaken the douche button for the flush, and water had sprayed all round the cubicle. She naturally wanted to leave a good impression, so she wiped the seat, the walls and the floors with tiny, thin pieces of tissue.

Another flight attendant trying to flush a public toilet in Japan set off the fire alarm at a shopping center. She fled the scene when four security guards entered the room.

MATCHES AND STITCHES

A flight attendant entered a drugstore in New York, intending to buy some matches. "Could I have some stitches," she asked the cashier. The cashier gave her an odd look and asked her what she needed them for. "To light a cigarette?" my colleague suggested, and thought what business of hers was it anyway, when it suddenly hit her like a thunderbolt that the correct word was *matches*. She apologized, asked for matches and walked out hastily, pleading with the cashier to not tell anyone else.

Modern technology can sometimes take you by surprise. A young flight attendant was on a layover in London, and had no idea that her boyfriend had changed her cell phone settings so that the phone switched to local time automatically. There is a two-hour time difference between Helsinki and London. She woke up to her phone alarm, and was soon standing in the hotel lobby in full uniform at 3.30 am, waiting for the rest of the crew, thinking that they must be late because they had not received a wake-up call. Neither had she, and complained

about it to the receptionist. The receptionist asked her if she knew what time it was – their departure from the hotel would be two hours later.

Foreign currency can cause problems as well. At a 100-yen shop in Japan, a flight attendant was very surprised that the cashier did not accept the coins she had left over from her previous trip and now tried to pay with. She thought that the cashier was also surprisingly rude for a Japanese person, but just shrugged and paid with a credit card instead. She next tried to use her coins at Subway, but they were rejected again. The cashier was so embarrassed for her that he wouldn't take her card either, but just gave her the sandwich for free. Once the flight attendant was back at her hotel, she noticed that her coins were not Japanese yen, but Korean won. They didn't accept Hong Kong dollars in Bangkok either.

Nor is it any use to try and get cash with a hotel key card at an ATM.

When you do have the right currency with you, be careful in how you use it. A purser in India ordered the most expensive wine on the list, while the rest of us settled for something more moderately priced. "Well, when you've only got one liver, I guess you can ruin it with the good stuff," she shrugged.

"AND THIS IS NEW YORK CITY"

There is a definite upside to hotel life: there's always someone, who can help you. A flight attendant once called the reception to check what time it was. "Eight o'clock madam," was the reply. A minute later, she called again. "Is it 8 am or 8 pm?" she asked. "Eight o'clock am, madam," the patient receptionist replied. The flight attendant decided to go out for a walk, and called back again to check the temperature. Before she had time to ask anything else, the receptionist added, "And this is New York City."

You might not always get the kind of help you're hoping for. A flight attendant in New Delhi asked the female receptionist for directions to a shop that would sell feminine hygiene products. The receptionist was very kind and understanding, and said she would have some delivered. Relieved, the flight attendant returned to her room, and only a few minutes later, there was a knock on the door. An elderly gentleman in a white suit and turban held out a small silver tray, with a single tampon on it. I wonder which one of them was more embarrassed?

Another flight attendant found herself in an awkward situation, when she discovered a strange buzzing sound in her hotel room. The maintenance man came up to check, but could not think of a reason for the buzzing. The flight attendant moved to another room, but to her surprise, that room was buzzing too. The maintenance man began to wonder if the entire hotel was buzzing, and left to check if something could be done about it. In the mean time, the flight attendant realized that the buzzing came from her luggage: her electric toothbrush had pressed against something and switched on inside her suitcase.

There was a different kind of moving and shaking in New York hotel rooms in the 1970s. There was a coin slot next to the bed, and if you put a coin in the slot, the bed would begin to rock gently. Or so it should have. A flight attendant decided to give it a try, and slipped a coin in. The bed began to shake so hard that she could barely stay in it, let alone relax. The flight attendant spent a long time standing by the bed and waiting for the rocking to stop, so that she could get in it and get some rest.

Sometimes finding your room can be tough. In the old days, on a Zürich layover we would head straight out to the supermarket and buy some frozen escargots and other goodies unheard of in Finland. After a flight attendant returned from her shopping trip and got her room key, she was shocked to find a naked man lying on the bed. The man thought it to be a pleasant surprise. "Get in, lovely to have you here," he said. The flight attendant did a quick u-turn and returned to the lobby. A few minutes later, the man came down to the reception, this time half-dressed, and carrying the flight attendant's shopping bag. "You left so suddenly," he laughed. A few weeks later, the flight attendant had another layover in Zürich. The receptionist asked her if she preferred a room with or without a man this time.

Hotel keycards are not always 100% reliable, and we do occasionally try to enter the wrong room. You might realize this from a pilot's cap on the table, or a German tour operator's luggage tags. Sometimes the entire hotel can be wrong. Two colleagues were on a layover in Hong Kong, and returned to the hotel after dinner. The problem was they could not get their keycards to work. After several attempts, one of them realized, "Hey, we've changed crew hotels! We're staying next door."

"OLD FLESH KEEPS BETTER
AT A LOW TEMPERATURE"

Encounters at hotels can sometimes be unreal, as one crew experienced on their layover in Seattle. They were looking around at the pool feeling practically Lilliputian. As they began to wonder if the beer had shrunk them, they discovered that there was a "Talls meeting" at the hotel that weekend.

Another unreal incident occurred in Guangzhou, when North Korea's President Kim-Jong-Il was staying at the same hotel. Not all crew members had received the message in their rooms that they should keep their passports with them at all times due to tightened security. As crew members returned to the hotel after dinner, the ones without their passports were taken aside for questioning, while armed guards looked on. Finally the "criminals" were allowed to enter their rooms and take their passports out of the safety deposit boxes.

In Beijing, a flight attendant had an unusual visitor in her room. She woke up to a strange flapping sound. As she switched the light on, she discovered a bat flying about. The hotel personnel caught the intruder, but the rest of the crew teased the flight attendant about her flying visitor at breakfast.

Not everyone appreciates the food abroad. "You girls could have brought some Finnish yoghurt with you," commented a Finnish tourist in the elevator in Bangkok. "My stomach can't take the spices here."

Hotel air-conditioning is another hot topic (no pun intended). I knew a colleague, who would always set the air-conditioning on "high" in her room. "Why?" I once asked. "Old flesh keeps better at a low temperature" she replied.

THE BOYS DROP BY AT A TERRACE BAR

When you travel a lot, you can't avoid the occasional blunder. An active and curious person will get to see and do a lot. Flight crew are independent and self-directed, sometimes a bit too much so. This discovery was made by three pilots, who on their Osaka layover decide to go and find a nice terrace bar, since the weather was sunny and warm. The boys (we like to call pilots *boys*) had been walking along small winding streets in a residential area for quite a while, when they finally saw a small terrace with a table and three chairs. Perfect, they thought, sat down and ordered three Asahi beers. The waitress, an elderly lady, looked a little bemused, but replied "Hai," and soon brought the beers over. After a second round, the boys asked for menus. This time a man came over and explained in halting English that there were no menus, but he could cook something if they wanted to wait. At this point, it began to dawn on our pilots that they weren't actually sitting at a

restaurant, but in the old couple's backyard. The boys emptied their pockets of local currency and made a hasty exit, apologizing profusely.

In Delhi, a flight attendant woke up from her post-flight nap, and decided to go down to the reception and ask about restaurants that might be open. Unfortunately nothing was open yet, so the sleepy flight attendant headed back to her room. Somewhere from behind, a man rushed in front of her to hold the elevator doors open. She was grateful for the attention and pressed the button for her floor. "Then I realized that he hadn't held the door open for me, but Princess Victoria of Sweden, who had stepped into the elevator after me." The man was the princess's security guard, and eyed the flight attendant suspiciously. Moral of the story: Always, always, at least brush your hair before leaving the room, as you never know whom you might run into. And don't assume that men are holding elevator doors for you.

Sometimes, you need to be quite creative in order to get what you want. In the 1970s, we had longer layovers in New York, and used to go to the Village in the evening. The crew saw a long line, and wondered what was going on. As they had nothing to lose, someone suggested that they would show their Finnair ID cards and say, "Press". The trick worked, and the crew got to attend the 50th birthday concert of a famous singer. Occasionally, it pays off to be bold.

In Tokyo, our crew often had dinner at the "mother and son's" restaurant, which was a tiny place with only two tables. Sometimes, the mother would fold origami as presents for the crew. In turn, we would bring them souvenirs from Finland. Once, the son asked if our crew would like to participate in mikoshi celebrations the next day. A mikoshi is a divine palanquin that serves as a vehicle to transport a deity while moving between a main shrine and a temporary shrine during a festival. A few crew members accepted the invitation, and accompanied the boy on a rainy Sunday morning. They walked a long way until they reached the village. A canopy had been built on the village square, and there was a long table underneath it. The flight attendants were given yukatas to put on, and then they waited for the mikoshi to arrive. The mikoshi was a kind of decorated, wooden rectangle that stood on poles. The mikoshi bearers waved it from side to side and shouted. The flight attendants were placed at the back of the mikoshi, and as they were the tallest, they probably had the heaviest load to carry. The festivities lasted several hours, and whenever the flight attendants wanted to rest, the master of ceremonies would command them back to work.

There were a few organized breaks, when the men were given sake, and the flight attendants some Coca-cola. The procession passed a temple, and the flight attendants asked if they could go in. Permission was granted, and the women got to see the temple and its beautiful altar. Inside the temple, a Japanese man started talking to the flight attendants, and offered to teach them a Japanese prayer. He turned out to be a demanding teacher! Every time the women made a mistake in bowing or a Japanese word, he would make them start over. The situation was getting quite frustrating, and the flight attendants tired. Finally, the women were allowed to re-join the procession. Late at night, when the festivities were finally over, the flight attendants got their reward. Their dinner was packed in a small plastic container, accompanied by a bottle of beer each. All of the mikoshi bearers wanted to be photographed with the flight attendants – they were the first Europeans, and the first women, to participate in these festivities.

DOLLHOUSE

In Tokyo's perfumed dollhouse
  awaits a geisha, koto
  and green tea
spring flowers and the harvest moon.
Cursed be the night
  that makes the cherry blossoms bow.

Heavy masks at the theater,
doomed love on this Kabuki stage,
on which only the complaint
  of the crystal chandelier
  accompanies
a humbly kneeling neck.

Sirpa Kivilaakso

"KIMII, KIMII!"

Sometimes it's enough to be Finnish, discovered one flight crew in Japan, while waiting at the airport for their aircraft to arrive at the gate. Someone came to ask them where they were from. To the surprise of the crew, their reply set off a group of Japanese teenagers, who began crying and shouting. "Kimii, Kimii!" they shouted, and pulled out their cameras. The Japanese fans took dozens of photos of F1 driver Kimi Räikkönen's kinsmen.

Our crew have attracted attention is India as well. Once in Ahmedabad, a rickshaw driver pulled up at a gas station instead of going directly to the hotel. Surely a man-powered vehicle didn't need fuel? Not at all, for he had called all his friends and neighbors to come and admire the European women. Another motorcyclist was unlucky to collide with a rickshaw, as he stared at the tall, blonde flight attendants for a little too long. Ahmedabad is not a tourist destination, and you see very few foreigners there altogether. Finnair leisure flights used it as a place to re-fuel and change flight crew some years ago.

Finnair opened its Tokyo route in 1983. A few of our stewards had heard about geishas, and were interested in giving their services a try. At that time, Finnair flew to Tokyo only once a week, so the crew had time to do a lot of things while there. On the stewards' request, the hotel arranged for a geisha from a renowned geisha house. The geisha turned out to be about 70 years old, and she played a local instrument and sang. After her performance, she conducted a tea ceremony with all its minute details. I suppose the stewards didn't really feel that they got what they had hoped for, but bowed politely nevertheless – and paid a lot more than they had expected to. They had nothing left to live on for the rest of the week, while the other crew members thoroughly enjoyed their story.

New York flights used to change crew in Amsterdam. A flight attendant, who had just arrived from New York to Amsterdam, decided to go shopping. She tried on some jeans in a shop, but left, as she didn't really find anything she liked. A few blocks later, she realized she had a pair of jeans folded over her arm. Embarrassed, she hurried back to the shop, where the assistant was at least as surprised as the flight attendant.

A flight attendant went shopping in the terminal during the turnaround. She walked back to the aircraft, put her shopping bag in the cupboard, and sat down to wait for the cleaners in red uniforms to finish. She soon realized someone was staring at her. "Flying back to London with us?" asked one of the "cleaners". The flight attendant had walked into the wrong plane!

The young flight attendant, who had just come back to work from mother's leave, had no idea what she was getting into, when she joined the rest of the crew for a day out in Tenerife. The crew decided that she should participate in a beauty contest, which was to start within minutes. She needed a little convincing, but finally agreed, borrowed a swimsuit from the hotel and put it on. Backstage, girls were getting their makeup done by professionals, and mothers were giving their daughters final words of advice. The other girls were nervous and shaking, so the flight attendant took on a motherly role, and even offered to go on stage first. The stage was lit brightly, a band was playing, and the rest of the crew cheered the flight attendant on. Of course "Catharina from Finland" won the contest and brought home a huge trophy, to the amazement of her tennis player husband, who was usually the one to bring the trophies home.

WORKING ON HOLIDAY, AND IN CIVILIAN CLOTHES

Sometimes flight attendants find themselves having to work even on holiday, as did a steward, who was returning from his first Caribbean cruise in 1991. The ship docked in Miami on Saturday morning, and the steward rushed to the airport. When he got there, he was told that Eastern Airlines had gone bankrupt, and all of its flights had now been cancelled. This of course meant that all other flights out of Miami would be overbooked for weeks. The steward started to get a little nervous, as he was supposed to be on a flight to Tokyo on Monday evening. He headed to the Continental Airlines counter, where he noticed the same beautiful employee, Candy, who had escorted him on to a flight to Denver two weeks earlier. Candy remembered him, and asked him

where he was going. Candy said that he had no hope of getting on a flight as an ID passenger, especially since he was the employee of another airline. The steward asked if he had even the slightest chance to get a place on a jumpseat, as he had to get to New York. Candy paused to think, and then asked him to contact Continental's Crew Control, which was just behind the corner. The controller called three aircraft that were bound for New York. The hopeful steward heard the captain at the other end ask whether he was cabin or cockpit crew. When the steward said that he was cabin crew, the controller gave him a form to fill, and said that flight 880 would take him, as long as he was willing to work on board! Naturally, the steward agreed. He was relieved that he'd worn a white shirt and dark trousers, as it would help him fit in. When he got on board, the captain checked his ID and qualifications. The purser, who introduced himself as Jim, said that one of the flight attendants had food poisoning and could not work, but wanted to go back to New York. Therefore, the crew would need help in the forward galley during the flight. The steward stayed in the galley, preparing meal trolleys, making coffee, and otherwise helping with the service. There were 20 passengers in first class and over 100 in economy, and none of them were to find out that he was an outsider. "It was quite an experience, to be working in civilian clothes on a Continental Airlines flight from Miami to New York," said the steward later. They landed in New York on schedule. The captain handed him back his unused ticket, and the purser gave him a bottle of champagne and some red wine to take along. The Continental crew was grateful for the help, and the steward was relieved to be able to make it home on time. The world was a different place back then.

Culture and language obstacles create a multitude of situations onboard aircraft. When both parties mean well, but do so according to their own behavioral norms, the result is often unintentionally comical. On a flight to Japan, the travel agency had upgraded an elderly couple from the countryside to business class. The crew and the couple did not have a language in common. The flight attendant serving the passengers bowed and smiled, bowed and smiled. At some point, the couple had had enough food, but did not know how to express this. Finally the woman waved her hand, smiled widely and said, "Get lost!"

Japanese passengers are very close to our hearts, and we often wonder about the right way to behave with them. Japanese rules for polite conduct are so different from European ones that sometimes we tend to worry too much, as did a recent recruit on a flight to Paris. There was a large group of Japanese passengers onboard, and the flight attendant tried to recall what she had been taught in her training. Could she look them in the eyes, how low should she bow, how wide should she smile, and should she serve the man or the woman first? Just after takeoff, a European passenger pressed the call bell. The flight attendant went to check what he wanted, but the aircraft passed through some turbulent weather, and the flight attendant lost her balance. She grabbed a seatback for support, and held on to it while she spoke with the customer. When she was done, she turned around and noticed to her horror that she was not holding on to a seatback, but the bald head of an elderly Japanese man. She had not been able to tell the difference with her gloves still on. She panicked, as she did remember having been taught that the top of the head is sacred for the Japanese, and you should never, ever touch it.

Often when you don't have a common language with a passenger, sign language can prove helpful. However, even gestures leave space for ambiguity. A man came into the rear galley on the DC-10; he was speaking, rolling his head around, and doing some sort of stretches. Even a lesser gifted person would see that he wanted a place to exercise. I gestured to the wide space he was standing in, smiling and nodding, "Go right ahead." After minutes of more gesturing, twisting and turning, I finally understood that the wanted to change his trousers. Clearly the place I suggested wasn't ideal.

A BARGAINING SMOKER

Smoking used to cause a lot of questions and bargaining on flights. Even in the 1990s, it was still common for Russian passengers to offer us money, expecting that to grant a permission to smoke.

The formalities for entering Russia were hard to handle for some passengers. "Why is it so hard to get into Russia?" asked a frustrated American woman filling in immigration and customs forms. "Foreigners fill in exactly same kind of forms when entering the United States," I said. The woman was clearly surprised. "Yes, but that's understandable," she remarked.

Hygiene standards vary from country to country, as one of our flight attendants noticed on a trip to China. She passed a restaurant that looked nice, and decided to go in. The place looked clean, there were white tablecloths on the tables, and she was greeted in a friendly manner. The waiter took her to a long table with other diners, and she managed to order some food and a Coca-cola. She politely declined the tea that was offered. The meal that she had ordered looked and tasted delicious. At some point, three diners paid and left the table. Others came in and took their place, and the flight attendant soon stopped smiling. The cups or chopsticks were not replaced. Instead, the patrons rinsed the dishes in a bowl that was at the centre of the table – with tea. The flight attendant decided it was time to go, and hoped and prayed she would not catch anything fatal. She was lucky indeed, or then all the other customers were healthy, as she did not fall ill after the visit.

After the disintegration of the Soviet Union, there were a lot of immigrant families on Finnair flights to New York. Usually they had a potty with them, and the children would do their business right their on the aisle. Who cares, if the cabin crew were serving meals at the time?

Even if cultural differences cause surprise, confusion, or uncertainty, we are always richer after encountering them. It's important to remember that there are no better or worse cultures, but only different ones.

FLYING TRENDSETTERS

If you know flight attendants, you will probably know the recent trends in clothes, toys and interior design, and if they don't know about them yet, they will find out very soon! Not only because they are genetically programmed to shop anywhere and everywhere, but also because flight attendants know how to prioritize their free time. Why waste time on shopping in your home town, when you can do so somewhere else? This way, you have more time for your family, hobbies, studies and social life, which often suffer because you're away so much.

Even though layovers are shorter and shorter, there might still be time to find birthday presents for your children or god children. You can shop for affordable hygiene products, for example "the best toothpaste in the world" in New York. You might find just the basketball shoes your son wants at a sale, or a unique Christmas present for your mother-in-law. This way, you can save time, energy, your nerves, and sometimes even money. Not always, but we try…

Flight attendants often bring food from their trips. Sometimes the world's best pizza from New York will find its way to a flight attendant's suitcase and on to the dinner table at home. Her children are happy, and she's happy being able to skip a trip to the supermarket after a long flight – a true win-win situation!

Sometimes you just can't find what you need, or you find what you don't need, or really even want. A purchase may have been a good idea at the time, or this or that item fit perfectly. Colors look different in different countries. I've occasionally brought the odd multi-colored duvet or tablecloth home, only to find them too loud for my apartment.

We can draw the conclusion that you can't win all the time. Besides, there's always your basement or garage, the flea market, or your friends and colleagues, to whom you can sell or donate clothes that don't fit. Flight attendants donate a lot to the Salvation Army and other charities. Nobody is as creative in buying, storing and recycling things as a flight attendant!

CREW STORIES

DURING THE TURNAROUND in Monastir, a bird cage vendor would always show up at the rear door of the Caravelle. For a long time, I regretted not buying one so much that eventually I had to get one in Guangzhou, China. I now have absolutely no use for it whatsoever.

WE USED TO bring these small chain saws from New York in the 1970s. First, you had to buy a Marimekko canvas bag from Finland, since it was just the right size for transporting it, and of course they would never guess at customs what you had inside it.

WHEN WE STILL had a stop in Amsterdam on the way to New York, the inbound crew would always tell the outbound crew what to buy. Once, a steward and I decided to invent a product that didn't exist. So, when we got to Amsterdam, we told the crew that we had found a wonderful bargain: a honey pump! The steward explained in great detail where to find this honey pump, and what it cost with and without the VAT. People talked about the honey pump for a long time, but nobody ever managed to find one. They must have been sold out…

In the 1970s, everyone had to get Nina Ricci's L'Air du Temps perfume from Hamburg, where a vendor came to the aircraft. A few years later, the perfume of the day was Guerlain's Shalimar, which we bought in Amsterdam. Then came Estée Lauder's White Linen, which we got in New York, of course.

WE WERE SHOPPING in Athens with a colleague, when a shopkeeper, small man, waved to us, and urged us to enter his shop. Soon, he brought over some tea and Metaxa. We spent a long time in that shop. My colleague had her eye on a mink coat, of all things, but said she didn't have enough cash on her to buy it. The shopkeeper told her not to worry; he took down her name and address, and handed her the coat. We left the shop with our heads spinning, but my colleague did go back another day, and paid for the coat. This is what shopping was like in Greece in the 1960s; even back then, Finns had a good and reliable reputation.

HEAD BUGS

A STEWARD, WHO loved all kinds of beautiful and interesting objects, once bought a large wooden head from some exotic destination. He was very proud of his find, and placed it in the living room.

Having returned from yet another long trip, he flung himself down on the couch, and the jolt caused a leg to break from under the head – or so he thought. Closer inspection revealed that the wooden head was infested with termites, which were slowly chomping away at the wood. The steward was immediately disenchanted with the souvenir, and threw it out as fast as he could.

A COLLEAGUE ONCE told me that she collected all kinds of things, and was a very impulsive shopper. She had a special storage room at home, she said, full of lovely things she had bought. Sometimes she just carried her shopping bags in from the car and straight into her storeroom. She didn't even remember buying everything that was in it, but they were all must-have items: Tiffany lamps, dhurrie rugs, paintings from Cairo, even one or two answering machines. She would shut the door quickly, if the stacks of items grew too high and something was about to fall down. She didn't think it was a problem, though, as you never know – one day those things might be invaluable.

I WENT SHOPPING for carpets somewhere in Asia. I bought three different ones, and was very happy with them at the time. However, once I got home, I began to regret my hastiness. I put two of

JETLAG CLOTHES

I stare in wonder
at these shopping bags
full of clothes
that can't be mine.
Luckily I have
a jetlag lipstick to match.

Riitta Kiiveri

the carpets in the living room, but for one of them it was only a brief visit, and the third is still rolled up in my garage, as it has been since the day I brought it home.

IN FINLAND IN the 1990s, only pharmacies sold effervescent vitamin tablets. I looked on in wonder as a first officer stocked up on them in Zürich. "Oh, they're very handy," he explained, "I make drinks with them. I just put some vodka, water and one of these tablets in a glass. There's no need to carry heavy cartons of juice to the summer cottage." Yes, handy indeed.

SOME TIME BACK in the 1980s, everyone bought Levis 501 jeans in New York. They had a low waist and didn't suit me at all, but of course I had to buy several pairs in different colors, since every-one else had them. Once someone took a picture, in which all of us flight attendants were wearing these jeans. I took one look at it, and got rid of my 501s for good.

AT SOME POINT, everyone bought earrings at Linn's silver shop in Bangkok. They had a blue or a transparent stone on them, and they were popular among our crew for years. About 10 years ago, you could always pick a Finnair flight attendant from the crowd by her Longchamp holdall. In Beijing, the vendors would recognize you a mile away, which was a good thing, in a way, as it saved you the trouble of haggling. "Yes, yes, I know you know what to pay," they would pretend to grumble, and still overcharge us.

WHEN WE FLEW to the United States with the DC-8 in the 1960s and 1970s, our layovers were long, and the trips quite frequent. We always had to look well-groomed, so to make life easier, we bought these kanekalon wigs in the U.S. Everyone had them at the time. They were not only handy to wear, but also good for smuggling foreign currency. We would hide cash inside the wig, and for example, buy Hungarian zlotys in Vienna, and then buy goose liver with the money in Budapest. Sometimes the Finnair proverb "Nobody is as clever as a flight attendant" rings true!

CHAPTER 13

ENCOUNTERS

HAVING FLOWN FOR decades, a flight attendant will have met thousands of people. Some of them, they will never forget.

One good example is a tall man, who got on among the last passengers on a flight from New York to Helsinki. He was wearing funny, large shoes, and he had a clown's nose on a string around his neck. I looked at his shoes, and said, "You have very interesting shoes." "I have gout," the man replied, smiling mischievously. "Of course, that's what I thought too," added the flight attendant. The passenger turned

out to be the doctor and hospital clown Patch Adams, whose life story was first published as a book and then made in to a Hollywood film, starring Robin Williams. During the flight, Patch Adams told me about the important work that hospital clowns do, especially with children, who are seriously ill, or have been through a lot in countries struck by war. Patch's home was the whole world. A clown can bring love closer.

At the end of the flight, the lovely Patch took my hand and said, "You'd make a good clown," and gave me the address of his website. Why not, I thought, maybe one day.

CREW STORIES

I THINK THIS happened in the mid 1990s. We were busy with our pre-flight duties, when the RC came in, asking that we reserve the first row. A person of high status, who did not want any special attention, had been given some special attention, and him and his entourage would be seated on the first row. The passengers came in, and last of all, our "VIPs". We shook hands, and they sat down quietly. The flight to Zürich could begin. Our VIP had a warm smile, and he was very interested in Finland and our work, as he had not met many Finns before. He admired the beautiful winter scenery outside. When we got to Zürich, he thanked us for the kind service and conversation, and wished us a peaceful life and time at work. Nelson Mandela continued his journey on another airline, to another part of the world. It was our pleasure to share a little part of his journey.

ONE NIGHT IN BANGKOK

My eyes sting
from exhaust fumes
– is this the intoxicating drug
  of humid Bangkok nights?

At a familiar street corner
  the idle sleep.

On the dark side of the alley
  I throw a dime
  out of pity
  to a begging hand
  and think I'm washing mine.

Sirpa Kivilaakso

"ME, OLD BLACK MAN?"

LOUIS ARMSTRONG WAS touring in Finland in the 1970s. I closed the curtain between the first class and economy, so that our famous passenger could have some privacy. The other passengers had seen Armstrong, and were trying to get a chance to talk to him. I told the singer that he was in great demand. "Me, old black man?" he replied modestly.

A FAMOUS SPORTS coach was traveling in economy class on a night flight from Bangkok to Helsinki. Most of the passengers were asleep, but the coach came to the rear galley to chat. He had written many books about coaching, team work and helping people, both at work as well as in their leisure time. We talked about our wellbeing, handling stress and exhaustion. We both had experience on how difficult it was to try and lift oneself out of depression. We also talked about how hard it was to adjust to big changes at work. This was a very significant encounter for me; one of the reasons why I've managed to fly this long, I think.

THE FAMOUS JAZZ singer Ella Fitzgerald received bad reviews for her concert in Helsinki. On the flight, Ella asked the purser if there were any reviews on her performance in the Finnish newspapers. The purser only told her the good news, as she didn't want to disappoint the artist. This purser used to work as a trainer too, and always emphasized the importance of being positive.

Photo by: Harri Erho

CHAPTER 14

JETLAGGED

WE CROSS SEVERAL time zones on long-haul flights. We return home often already on the next day, and wait for our body and mind to meet again. If you can't get a good night's sleep at some point during the trip, one time zone-crossing flight equals three nights of lost sleep altogether. We might have two to five of these flights in total per month. For that reason, sleep is very important to us.

When we wake up to head home from Asia, it is midnight in Finland, and we occasionally wonder whether our skin would benefit more from day or night cream. Somehow, the work gets done, sometimes "on autopilot", but once we get home, we let go. You might still think that you're doing fine, but experience has proved that the elevator doesn't go all the way up, which can be a difficult combination: your limbs are working, but your brain is asleep. Your reaction speed equals a moderate state of drunkenness, and your memory is as good as a carrot's. What's most deceiving is that you might not feel sleepy, but actually, the lights are on and nobody's home. This half-coma generates situational comedy, which the main character usually doesn't get until he or she has had a good night's sleep.

CREW STORIES

AT THE SUPERMARKET, I found it irritating that my husband constantly ran away with the shopping trolley when I was trying to put something in it. Finally, I realized that the man I was following was actually not my husband, and my own beloved was staring at me in shock from the other end of the aisle.

IT STARTED RAINING on my drive home. I pulled up in my driveway, and as I was reaching for my handbag from the next seat, I knocked over a water bottle that was in the cup-holder. I pulled my umbrella out of the bag, accidentally opening it inside the car. I pushed my cell phone against the seat, and it beeped, probably sending an empty text message to someone. With my other hand, I somehow managed to press the car key, the boot snapped opened and my sunglasses fell off my forehead. All this happened within seconds! I was angry at first, but then I couldn't help laughing. They say that lack of sleep hampers your coordination. I'll say!

I DROVE INTO the car wash and was suddenly aware of someone knocking on the window. I opened the window and asked if the man knew how dangerous it was to be inside a car wash while it was operating. Apparently I'd been sleeping in the car for 45 minutes.

I WAS ON my way home after a night flight, and needed to stop at the pet shop. The shop wasn't open yet, so I parked outside to wait. My next recollection is that some very worried-looking people are knocking on the windows and shouting. I'd slept clutching the wheel, with my head thrown back and drool running down my chin. Clearly the passers-by had thought that I was having some kind of seizure.

I HAD BOOKED a vet's appointment for my dog straight after a long-haul flight. I was half-way to the clinic, when I realized that I had forgotten the dog at home…

I HAD PARKED my car outside in the staff parking lot, and it had snowed 20 centimeters. I didn't have a brush or gloves with me. I cleaned the windows and the roof of the car with my bare hands. When I got to the rear window, I was amazed to find a rear window wiper. My car didn't have one…

I TOOK A nap after a New York flight, and woke up somewhat confused when my mother called. "How was New York?" she asked. "I wasn't in New York; I was at the countryside with a friend." I have no recollection of that call, and my mother was somewhat surprised when I called her later on the same day, saying, "Greetings from New York!"

THE LARGE-SCALE
CONSUMER'S SHOPPING TROLLEY

 A COLLEAGUE TOLD me once how she had provided some amusement to her fellow shoppers at the supermarket, as she absent-mindedly pushed around a promotional shopping trolley full of toilet paper rolls. "When you gotta go, you really gotta go," one of the other shoppers remarked.

ONCE AFTER A Bangkok flight, I went to pick up my children from daycare, only to find that they weren't there! They were sick, and my parents were at home looking after them. "Right, I knew that!" You should have seen the expressions on the teacher's face.

I HAD FORGOTTEN to set my cell phone to local time after I got back from Bangkok. I set the alarm for the next morning, and was really upset that the newspaper was late. It was 2.30 am, and my husband walked me back to bed.

IT'S SO IRRITATING to wake up and not know if it's 7 am or pm.

ONCE AFTER SEVERAL long days at work, I finally had a day off, and decided to go to the gym. I was nearly at the airport, when I realized where I was going.

A FEW YEARS ago, I came home after a flight from Toronto that was several hours delayed, and decided to take a nap. When I woke up, it was nearly 10 o'clock, but the problem was that I had no idea whether it was 10 in the morning or evening. The weather was dark and gray. I decided to check if the

JET LAG

For 24 hours my home is
a room, a TV, a bed and a WC
on the 42nd floor,
with a view of the backyard.

The whole night
I'm in a waking dream
I lie and listen
to my crackly shell
that sleeps in the smooth sheets
of my replacement home,
as my body clock ticks
* somewhere over the Atlantic*
and my thoughts run away
- My dear, don't run!

How much of life remains unlived
as I stretch to the tempo of jetlag
here and there
* - in a waking dream -*
watching
the turbulence of my thoughts
on the mirrored walls.

Sirpa Kivilaakso

newspaper had come – if it had, it was Tuesday morning, and if not, it was still Monday evening. The Tuesday paper had indeed been delivered, and I had slept 18 hours instead of taking a short nap.

 I FORGOT MY infant daughter at the bank, and was nearly home when I realized what I'd done. I drove back, and there she was, on the rocking-horse where I'd left her... The bank-teller looked horrified, and I didn't tell my husband until perhaps 10 years later. My daughter wasn't in the least bit traumatized, though, as she later became a flight attendant herself. She says that she remembers it, but wasn't worried, because she knew I'd come back eventually... I always did.

I CAME TO work by car, but took the bus home, which I didn't realize, of course, until I was already at home.

I LOOKED FOR my car in the outdoor parking lot, and even brushed the snow off a few cars until I realized that my husband had driven me to work that day, and I was supposed to get a taxi home.

I STOPPED THE car to look for the car keys that maybe fell out of my handbag, when I was looking for the car keys... No, wait... What was I doing?

I FORGOT TO put the handbrake on when I parked the car, and in the morning, I found my car backed into the neighbor's spruce hedge. It had slid neatly across the street, and managed to find the only lamppost in the hedge.

I LEFT THE trash bag by the front door, intending to take it out on my way to the supermarket. When I got back from the shop, I realized I had forgotten to take the trash out. I left the shopping bag in the hall, and took some recyclable newspapers and the trash bag out. When I got back, I started unpacking the shopping, and realized that somehow, this was the trash bag.

AS I WAS out walking the dog, I noticed a pair of pantyhose, and then a sock. "That's funny," I thought, until I saw that a matching sock was half-way out of my own pant leg.

WHY ON EARTH WOULD
SOMEONE GO SHOPPING IN THEIR UNIFORM?

I CAME HOME after a Bangkok flight. I made porridge for the children, and sent them off to school. The place was a mess – maybe I should just wipe these counters? Perhaps I should vacuum-clean? Might as well wash the windows too... Oh, look at the time, I better go to the supermarket... "Why on earth would someone go shopping in their uniform?" I wondered, until I realized I was looking at my own reflection.

I DROVE TO the supermarket after a long-haul flight, and once I was done, sat in the back seat. I sat and waited there for a few minutes, until I realized that I had come to the supermarket alone, and would therefore have to do the driving.

I GOT ON a tram after returning from Shanghai, exhausted from the flight, and dragging my trolley bag and suitcase with me. As I clambered on the tram, my other shoe fell off. I was so tired I couldn't care less, and decided to just leave it there, as I didn't have a long way to go. A man picked it up for me and followed me on to the tram. "Excuse me, I think you dropped a shoe?" he asked. "Yeah, whatever, thanks." I replied. A tram load of people stared at me like I was a half-wit, not to mention rude. I was embarrassed then, and embarrassed now.

There are many stories involving lost crew bags – not lost by the airline, but by ourselves. Fortunately, there's usually a responsible first officer to keep an eye on everyone's luggage, and locate it for you when you don't recognize it or remember having it with you, and at home, friendly neighbors will usually return your suitcase when you leave it standing alone in the parking lot.

I WOKE UP to the sound of the buzzer. What the... didn't people understand that I'd been working all night and needed to sleep? "What!" I barked into the intercom. "I was just wondering if that black suitcase in the driveway is yours... It has a crew tag and your name on it?" asked my neighbor. "Oh...Yes, it's mine," I sighed. I guess I'd left it there, when I went to take out the trash that I'd forgotten to take out three days earlier. You know – the usual jetlag stuff.

WHEN I GOT back from the supermarket, I felt like I'd left something behind...the dog! I'd left the poor thing leashed outside the entrance, and taken a different exit.

I THOUGHT I was feeling fine after a flight home from China, and decided to go to the grocery store by bike. As I was trying to pick some potatoes, I realized it had been a bad idea, as it was hard to do any shopping and walk the bike and the same time...

I USED TO do some extra shifts at a pharmacy when I first started flying. As a customer came in, I walked up to him, welcomed him onboard, and asked if I could be of any assistance.

I CALLED MY husband after a long-haul flight, asking him to call me, so that I could find my cell phone by its ringtone. My husband laughed, and asked which phone I might be calling from...

"MOM, GO TO BED!"

MAUNO KOIVISTO WAS the president at the time, and I'd just returned from New York. The children announced: "Mom, you're so tired, you should go to bed!" "No, I'm fine," I insisted, having missed my children. "No, you're not," said my daughter. "Yes, I am," I repeated. "Ok, who's the president?" asked my son. "Silly, it's Mauno Kuusisto!" Nice try – Mauno Kuusisto was a singer.

A LONG TIME ago, I decided to stop by at the grocery store on my home from work. I bumped into one of our pilots in the shop. He happened to be married to a colleague, who had been on a layover in Bangkok at the same time as I, but as a member of a different crew. We had slightly different schedules, so she was coming back a few days later. I explained to the man what a lovely time we'd had wit his wife, and how lucky she was to get to stay an extra day or two in the sun. I thought the husband seemed a bit distant – and what was he wearing! Well, men get a bit strange-looking if left alone too long, I concluded, went home and took a nap. After I woke up, I realized I'd forgotten to buy all kinds of items, and had to go back for more groceries. Pilot X was there again! Only what was he doing cutting meat in a white coat behind the counter? I had been pouring my heart out to the shopkeeper, whom I had earlier mistaken for one of our pilots in my confused condition. I had to explain. The shopkeeper laughed it off, and said, "I don't know your colleague, but I'm glad you ladies had a good time!"

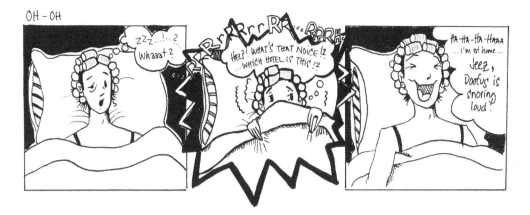

OH - OH

 I WAS WALKING downtown with my mother, when we passed a colleague I knew, so I smiled and said hi, and he said hi back. "Just a colleague," I explained to my mother. "No, it wasn't," she said, "That was the anchorman of the 10 o'clock news."

I'D COME BACK from Narita, and was feeling surprisingly energetic, so I decided to go out for a run. I double-checked that I had my house keys with me. I heard them clinking in my pocket. When I got back from my run, I noticed that I had some change in my tracksuit pocket, and my keys were inside the house.

MORE TYPICAL SITUATIONS:

- You come home and lock the car, but you're still sitting in it.

- You're on you cell phone with a friend, but you tell her you need to end the call because you think you've forgotten your cell phone on the aircraft.

- You try to open your front door with your Finnair ID card.

- You pay your groceries and leave them at the store.

- Your trolley bag is still out in the hall, and your suitcase is blocking the driveway.

- You leave your grocery shopping on the dining table, and put your keys and purse in the fridge.

- You knock on the door of your bathroom, even though you're home alone.

- You take your trolley bag and suitcase inside, and then have a shower. You then start looking for your handbag, which you find in the hallway.

- You sit down on a chair and start looking for a seatbelt.

- You collect your cash at the ATM, and politely bow and say "thank you" to the great amusement of the next person in line.

- You go and have a shower, and notice you still have your handbag on your shoulder.

- You have a doctor's appointment and announce to the receptionist, "I have an appointment at one with Captain Virtanen."

- You notice you've taken your colleague's suitcase by mistake, and return it. Her building doesn't have an elevator, and she lives on the fourth floor. Then you drive back to the airport to collect your own suitcase.

- You're about to leave the house, but can't find the keys anywhere. They've been hanging in the lock since you opened the door eight hours earlier.

- You decide to take the trash out on your way to the supermarket. At the supermarket, you notice that you're still carrying the trash bag.

- As you put lip balm on, you wonder why it's so sticky. Oops, it's glue.

Sounds familiar?

CHAPTER 15

THE JOY AND SORROW OF STANDBY DUTY

STANDBY – FORCED misery or excitement and pleasant surprises? Flight attendants are occasionally on standby, to cover for crew members that are sick, roster changes due to weather conditions or technical problems, and other last-minute changes. Standby raises all kinds of emotions and not least because on a several-day stand by period, you might be sent on a long-haul trip, a domestic layover, or a sequence of short-haul flights. You never know in advance, but you have to be prepared. Will I need a woolen hat or a bikini? Who's looking after the children and for how long? What about the dog?

Crew Control makes the calls to cabin crew on standby and assigns them on flights. You get used to being on standby… or you don't. Some find standby duty refreshing, as it brings an element of surprise into their lives, others are stressed, even if they've been flying for years. One experienced colleague says that she is ready and waiting by the phone with her bags packed, already before her standby starts. The situation seems to worsen for the nervous ones as they get older; soon they'll be sitting in the car and waiting. Whether we like it or not, we all occasionally have standby, which increases unpredictability in our lives that are irregular to begin with.

Crew controllers have told me that people occasionally answer, "No! I'm not going to f***ing London!" Some destinations are clearly more popular than others. However, the most frequent comment we make is, "When am I coming home?"

CREW STORIES

⏰ **I WALKED AROUND** in circles, cell phone in my pocket, all made up and no place to go. I added some powder every now and then, and did pull-ups every hour. I checked several times that my phone was on. I confirmed from my roster that I had the right day and time. Everything was in order, but there was still no call. I didn't get round to doing the laundry or ironing clothes, what with having to be ready all the time. By the time my standby ended I was so tired I had to take a nap.

"DID WE WAKE YOU?"

⏰ **THIS HAPPENED WHEN** Crew Control headquarters were still at the Crew Center. I woke up to the phone ringing at five past six in the morning. "Did we wake you?" asked a familiar voice at the other end. "It's Crew Control, good morning! We have some work for you." "Er... what kind of work?" I asked. "Well, you'd be serving passengers food and drinks... Actually, would you be willing to go on a prop plane flight to Calgary?" By this time, I was fully awake. "Calgary as in Canada? With a prop plane..." "Yes, I know it sounds unusual," admitted the controller. I began to calculate how many nights we'd have to be away, and how much money I would make! Suddenly there was a loud noise at the other end, as practically everyone working at Crew Control was doubling up with laughter. "You're not going to Calgary, go back to bed!" I heard my friend's voice on the line. He had decided to play a little prank at my expense. I didn't find it very funny at the time.

ROAMING

I am lost on the streets
  of the world
in time away from myself.
Soft massaging hands
keep me alive
from one trip
to another,
as my feet shout for salvation
and my heart beats
with the uneven surface
  of these city streets
these streets,
this night.

Riitta Kiiveri

⏰ **WE USED TO** have a telephone on my husband's bedside table. It rang at 4.01. "Who the h*** is calling at this hour!" my husband yelled, and hung up the phone. "No, don't, I'm on standby!" I said. I was very embarrassed to answer a second call from Crew Control. "Oh, don't worry," said the controller. "We've heard all sorts."

🕐 **I WAS ON** standby and my five-year-old daughter asked me, if I was going to work. I said I was already working, in a way: I was on standby in case someone falls ill. "Yes, and then you'll go and look after them," said my daughter.

🕐 **A BEAUTIFUL AND** experienced flight attendant, whose sense of self-worth was rather well-developed, got a call from Crew Control. She was asked to do a domestic flight. "In your dreams, honey!" she replied. Domestic flights were for junior crew – at least in her opinion.

CHAPTER 16

EXCITEMENT IN THE AIR

EVERY FLIGHT IS different. You never know if you're going to be facing a bag full of snakes or an aggressive passenger. A flight attendant's loved ones might also get palpitations from a phone call from Finnair Crew Control. Alcohol consumed from one's own bottle on a flight can raise the blood pressure of both the passenger and the cabin crew.

CREW STORIES

WE WERE ON our way to the United States on a DC-8, and perhaps about half-way over the Atlantic, when a drunken man came out of the forward toilet. He grabbed my hand and whispered, "There's a snake in the toilet." I think I replied something along the lines of, "Yeah, right," but the man insisted he was serious, so I followed him to the toilet. A snake was curled up in the middle of the toilet floor. Its neck was outstretched, and it was hissing threateningly. I locked the door and went to tell the captain. We first tried to tranquilize the snake by spraying air freshener in its eyes, which only made it angrier. Finally, we taped a fire axe on the captain's hand with duct tape, and left him in the toilet with the snake. The captain chopped the snake up in to tiny pieces. We sent the pieces to Helsinki to be identified, but we never found out what kind of snake it was, or where it could have come from.

 AT SOME POINT it was very fashionable in the new World to buy items from the Old World for the sake of continuity. One

Finnish immigrant had made a significant fortune in the United States, and to highlight his roots, had bought a stone church – apparently not a whole building, but its foundation stones. According to the aviation authority, the distance from the cockpit to the rear part of the aircraft was too long, so a flight attendant had to accompany the pilots for safety reasons. Somewhere over the Atlantic Ocean, I thought to myself how odd life was: you might get to serve kings and presidents, or sit in the solemn company of a stone church.

ON THE MD-80, in the earlier half of the 1980s, a male passenger called me over, opened a hidden compartment of his bag, and showed me what was in it: a slithering lump of tiny snakes! I was horrified, and made the man swear that not a single reptile would get out. The man seemed to enjoy shocking me. The snakes didn't escape, but I reported the incident, of course.

"THEY'RE NEVER GOING TO BELIEVE THIS AT WORK!"

BEFORE THE ERA of plastic cutlery, we used to have very sharp knives onboard, and the crew as well as passengers kept getting cuts. On a Boeing-757 leisure flight, once again a woman cut herself. She was seated in the middle seat, with her 10-year-old-son by the window, and her husband in the aisle seat. I brought the medical kit and took out the disinfectant. Either the sight of blood or the smell of the disinfectant was too much for the father, because he fainted, with his head on the meal tray. He didn't come to, so a colleague helped me to get him out of his seat. She unclasped his tight belt and elevated his legs. I sat on his chest (in my skirt) and undid a few buttons from his shirt. The man opened his eyes, assessed the situation, and said, "They're never gonna believe this at work!"

AS A YOUNG flight attendant, I still lived with my mother, and in those days Crew Control would call flight attendants' families to let them know if there was a significant delay. Once my mother received a call. "This is X speaking from Finnair Crew Control. Do you have a daughter named..." My mother's heart nearly stopped. The controller continued, "Her flight is two hours delayed."

A MAN, WHO had appeared to be in a good mood but was not too drunk, jumped up just before takeoff with the intention of going to the lavatory. He had the sense to sit down, but in the middle of the service, I heard loud noises from the rear part of the aircraft. The man was shouting and cursing the flight attendant for confiscating a bottle of alcohol, which he had nearly finished. A little later, he joined me in the forward galley, first raging at me, and then saying how lovely I was, and how good the service on the flight was. He then wanted to go to the toilet again, and started kicking the door, because he couldn't get it open. I opened the door for him. Then he couldn't get out, and started kicking the door. We helped him out, which inspired another angry tirade. The situation was threatening, so we notified Helsinki.

When he left the plane, the man smiled and thanked for the nice service! He had a connection flight to an Asian destination the same evening, but I doubt he was allowed to continue his journey.

AFTER TAKEOFF FROM London, we heard a strange noise from underneath the floor in the forward galley. We notified the cockpit of the situation, and the captain came out to check. There was a British woman seated on the first row, and she looked very frightened by what was going on. Some warning light came on in the cockpit, so our flight was diverted to Hamburg. The fire brigade had been notified, but the landing was perfectly normal. As soon as I had the chance, I went to talk to the frightened passenger. The man sitting next to her showed me his hand, which was red from having been squeezed hard, and possibly bitten. I said his hand looked like my husband's when I was giving birth to our first child. The man laughed and said that they didn't know each other, and she had just needed some support…

SINGAPORE SILK

The busy day of a vendor:
  – Copy watches, Mam!

The idle tourist's menu:
  – Singapore Sling and Hemingway
  On the terrace at Raffles
  sipping slowly…

The light afternoon drizzle
  decorates hats and souvenirs
  cameras and silks

If only one had time to use them all…

Sirpa Kivilaakso

PUTTING A PASSENGER'S laptop in the overhead locker for landing can trigger a sequence of events, which really require you to use your brain. I put a passenger's laptop in the wrong bag, and before anyone realized my mistake, the owner of that bag had left. I felt terrible. So I checked the Arrival Hall, went through the list of passenger with onward connections, called Arrival Services and Finavia, wrote e-mails in the middle of the night, and even drove to Hotel Kämp to deliver a message. I slept uneasily. The morning, however, brought good tidings: the owner of the bag had wondered about the extra laptop and contacted Finnair. I was then able to deliver the laptop to its rightful owner. I was so relieved! The moral of the story? Even if you screw up, you can still try to fix it!

I REMEMBER ONCE, when we got the hotel at our destination, the captain asked for the legendary "captain's suite". The receptionist replied that they have one on the top floor. "Ah, too bad," said the captain, "I never sleep higher than the third floor, in case there's a fire".

CHAPTER 17

FLORENCE FINNAIRGALE

EMERGENCY PROCEDURES AND first aid training are the most important areas in Finnair cabin crew training. Every flight attendant must know how to act in an emergency, as the main reason we are onboard is to ensure the safety of passengers.

CREW STORIES

IN THE OLD days, flying was even used as a health remedy. My sister had whooping cough, and the pediatrician "prescribed" a flight to Pori and back. For some reason, my sister's cough disappeared on the trip.

WHEN I FIRST started flying, I was very eager to practice my first aid skills. I had explained to my son, who was then eight years old, what resuscitation was. We were on a day cruise in the Turku archipelago, and sat inside on the way back, because it was a hot day. Half an hour before our arrival to Turku, a woman came in to ask if there were any medical personnel onboard. Nobody stood up, so I dug out my key ring, which had a resuscitation mask on it. I told my son I would go and see if I could be of any assistance. "Mom, you don't have to resuscitate here, it's only on the plane!" my son yelled. That time, someone had had an epileptic seizure, and there was no need to resuscitate anyone at all.

WE WERE ALREADY taxiing, when an elderly lady pressed the call bell. We went to see what the problem was. She said that she thought she might be having a heart attack. We went to get the purser, who had worked as a psychiatric nurse. The purser introduced himself, told her he was a psychiatric nurse, and asked if he could help her in any way. The woman appeared to recover quickly, as she said, "Oh, I'm fine now." Apparently she was just a nervous flier.

WE WERE ON our way home from the Canaries, when a man rushed into the forward galley, complaining of chest pain. We brought over an oxygen bottle and nitroglycerin. We put the patient in a half-sitting position, and gave him some oxygen. I tried to take down his details. Had he suffered from chest pain in the past? No, never, the man replied. Finally, the man told me he had eaten a lot of Canary potatoes and fried onions the night before… In other words, he had a lot of trapped gas in his stomach, and that caused the pain. A little while later, he managed relieve himself, which took the pain away immediately. I have since been teased for discovering the best cure for flatulence: nitroglycerin and oxygen!

A MALE PASSENGER fainted on the aisle. We made a PA for a doctor, and found one, who, without hesitation, punched the patient. We were horrified and told the doctor that it's not the way patients are treated on Finnair flights. The doctor replied that it was a standard procedure in Russia. To everyone's amazement, the patient came to, wondering why his jaw was hurting so much.

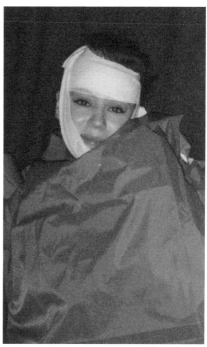

CHAPTER 18

AFTER RETIREMENT

ACCORDING TO AVIATION law, flight attendants in Finland have to hang up their wings latest at the age of 67. Many of us would like to continue even beyond that age, but most flight attendants retire at 60-63 years of age. Our work community is so tightly knit that we often wonder how we will survive without it. Then what? No more lovely colleagues, changing scenery, a hectic work pace with demanding customers, no layovers in exotic destinations with restaurants and shopping opportunities. The topic raises its head every now and then, and on many layovers we have tried to come up with the solution, which is a retirement home for ex-flight attendants called "Final Approach". A description of what the retirement home would be like will follow; but first, here are some facts to support it.

SENILITY... NO, SENIORITY NUMBER

When flight attendants first start out, their seniority is based on the date that they started working. Graduates from the same course would all have the same seniority number, so their internal order has to be determined. The internal seniority of a course used to be based on alphabetical order, but in 1996, the seniority has been determined by physical age, so that the oldest of the course is also the most senior. This seniority number is with us throughout our career, one way or another. The most senior flight attendant of the company is number 1, and if we employ 1650 flight attendants, the most junior would be 1650. As people quit or retire, your seniority number "improves", or grows smaller.

For example, someone who started flying in 1988, started out with the seniority number 1006, and is now, after nearly 25 years of flying, at 428. Since the beginning, seniority has affected bids for specific flights, and requests for days off and holidays, but less so today than in the past.

Our famous "free" tickets are not free at all. Seniority counts when you're travelling as an ID passenger. Finnair staff can travel on their stand by tickets if there are seats left over from paying customers, and can embark according to seniority, so that the most senior employees get the first free seats. ID travel can sometimes be a harrowing experience. Will there be any free seats? Do I have enough seniority?

FINAL APPROACH FOR
THE NATURALLY BEAUTIFUL

The retirement home for ex-flight attendants is located in a naturally beautiful place, on the shores of a lake with crystal-clear water, but still close to the centre of town. The compound has all the necessities: a shop, a massage parlor (with skilled masseurs and masseuses from Bangkok), tailors, saunas, indoor and outdoor swimming pools, and flower and herb gardens. Alcohol is available and delivered to your doorstep. All the facilities at Final Approach are accessible with wheelchairs and walkers. If you are confined to a wheelchair, you can pick an assistant from the talent list of a famous, international model agency.

Apartments at Final Approach are granted according to seniority, and not in the order you sign up for them. There is no way to jump the queue – not even if you pay. The apartments are of various sizes, from small studios to three-bedroom penthouses. You might be able to upgrade to a larger apartment when vacancies occur due to natural causes, but only if you have enough seniority. Your lease is granted only for a year at a time. Once a year, residents have to clear the residents' test, after which your lease can be extended. The resident's test is used to evaluate your suitability for Final Approach, and to brush up on your skills. For example, you must be able to empty a large glass of wine within 90 seconds. If you fail the residents' test, you need to practice, and retake the test on another day.

You are notified about meal times by telephone, just like Crew Control used to call you for work from standby. This way, residents can maintain a sense of self-worth and importance. The cafeteria at Final Approach is the replica of an MD-11 aircraft cabin, donated by Finnair.

After all, food tastes better in familiar surroundings. If you prefer, you can have your meal standing up in the rear galley next to the toilet, as that might feel more familiar to you. Should you choose the latter option, we make sure that someone uses the toilet all the time, to increase authenticity.

THE PURSER CHOOSES THE DESTINATION

Cafeteria staff is picked among residents for every meal service at Final Approach. If you have enough seniority, you are eligible to wait tables. The designated "purser" of each meal service can choose the "destination" and the menu. To start the meal, the staff on duty reminds everyone about the location of the nearest exits and toilets, and then the most junior retiree gives out newspapers, which have been left over from flights and are donated by Finnair Catering once a week. The meal service usually takes about three hours, since at Final Approach, there's no need to rush. In addition, the waiters are no longer all that quick or agile. The meals are prepared in the kitchen, and then placed on trays inside trolleys, unless they should happen to fall on the floor. The trolleys are specially designed, so that it is possible to push them even with a walker. Residents make announcements if they remember to. After the meal, the three most junior residents stay behind to clean and take care of the dishes. This way, we guarantee that residents stay active and feel useful.

In case someone is indisposed or unwilling to show up for their service duty that day, a resident is called from standby to cover. In addition, the retirement home has a sauna standby system, in case the residents would like to have it heated on short notice.

Various kinds of excursions are arranged for Final Approach residents, for example, visits to vineyards, breweries and local bars. The Final Approach residents' bus will pick up the participants from the main door at a set time. Residents must be on time, as the bus waits for nobody! The excursion participants must stay with their group at all times. All excursions have a dress code, a kind of uniform for residents

SMILING

She came smiling into the rear galley:
Such a wonderful airline
– hires older people.
How long have you been flying?
I smiled back:
Some thirty years
but only few long winters.

Riitta Kiiveri

to wear. It is strictly forbidden to bring overnight guests to Final Approach. If a resident should violate any of the rules listed above, they will be sanctioned – usually with indefinite standby duty.

There are daily visiting hours for residents' next of kin. They must book a visiting ticket in advance, and the price is 200 euro per person. The income is used for covering personnel costs (the wheelchair assistants). A maximum of 20 visitors are accepted per day. The visitors are allowed to enter based on the resident's seniority. If there are cancellations, visitors from a stand by list will be allowed to enter in order of resident seniority.

KARAOKE À LA THAILAND

Residents have a compulsory vacation of one week annually, when they must stay with their next of kin. This week is determined in advance according to a rotation system. It is forbidden to change the assigned week, even at the request of the resident's family.

There is a karaoke bar at Final Approach. It is located in an old potato cellar, with a dirt floor, wooden tables and benches, and dim lighting. The only available beverage is Singha beer, and the song lists only include Thai songs. To make the setting as authentic as possible, the employees are from Thailand, hired through a temporary employment agency. They don't speak any English or Finnish. The potato cellar is open every day, for as long as the patrons wish to stay.

Residents of this retirement home spend happy and joyful days filled with laughter together in an idyllic setting. Christmas, Midsummer, wedding and divorces are celebrated with equal enthusiasm; joys and sorrows are shared, just like they were on flights for all those years.

To conclude, here's a real life thought on retirement:

Two flight attendants, who were both close to retirement age, were talking about an early retirement package the company had offered them, when one of them remarked, "I've given this company my best years. Let it keep the rest too..."

CHAPTER 19

FLASH MOB, MOVEMBER, BOLLY-WOOD AND BLOGS

WHAT DOES IT mean to be cabin crew? Our purpose, first and foremost, is to ensure the safety of passengers. In fact, there is a saying among flight attendants, "We are not here to kiss your asses; we are here to save your asses." So, officially, we're *safety* professionals. Naturally, we are service professionals too, so that passengers would be more comfortable on their journey, the time would pass quicker, and they would not need to suffer hunger or thirst. Sometimes the slogan "Safety comes first, and everything else is show business" holds true, as there are plenty of talented, innovative, energetic and daring individuals among us.

A few of our creative and dynamic flight attendants had some brilliant ideas last year, and put these ideas into action by employing their big hearts, enormous zeal, long hours of voluntary work, a budget of zero, and a tremendous joy of doing. The Finnair cabin crew flash mob, the Movember campaign and the Bollywood dance on India's Republic Day charmed Finland and the rest of the world too, generating a lot of media attention. The cabin crew's Bollywood dance has so far had about 4.6 million hits on YouTube.

"I'M WEARING A MOUSTACHE FOR WORK TODAY"

Finnair Quality Hunter Thomas Spohn did not use to think that things happen for a reason, but after having to change to an earlier flight from

Helsinki to Berlin, he had "the most wonderful encounter ever" on a Finnair flight.

Thomas was not aware of the global charity campaign Movember, which involved growing a moustache in November, in order to raise awareness about prostate cancer and other men's health issues. Women could participate in the campaign too, but obviously had to be a bit more creative regarding facial hair.

Thomas was about to nod off, when he heard the following announcement by Purser Ami Niemelä:

"Ladies and gentlemen, would you agree that sometimes plunging in head first can bring better results than politically correct action? I firmly believe so, and for that reason, I find myself in this situation today. I promised my colleagues to wear a moustache for work today, if my account for the Movember campaign would receive 1,000 euro in total. I hope you won't be frightened by a flight attendant sporting a moustache, and kindly ask those of you with weak hearts to close your eyes now. I am doing this simply out of love for a man and all men. You will find more information about the Movember campaign in the Blue Wings magazine in your seat pocket. Thank you for your attention." Ami then appeared on the aisle, wearing a gray moustache she had made herself, and began serving customers.

Ami Niemelä has also collaborated with Helena Kaartinen in creating the Finnair flash mob and Bollywood dance event.

OM SHANTI OM

Helena Kaartinen was on Facebook one day, when a greeting from an Indian friend popped up on the screen. The friend in question was an ex-colleague and Bollywood dance instructor from Mumbai, Manish Gawde. "We chatted about this and that, and compared rosters," says Helena. I had some time off work, and nothing special planned. "Wow, take off and come here. Stay with us, and attend a course, or do volunteer work or something? Too many 'off' days doesn't suit you." Helena smiled, and recalled how another Indian had described his country:

in India, people speak different languages and eat different foods, but there is one thing in common for all parts of the country – hospitality.

Helena describes how her enthusiasm for the idea grew, and more words flowed on the screen. She tilted her head Indian-style in agreement, when Manish explained the importance of Bollywood for Indians. They discussed how dance was a universal language. Helena failed to mention how for some Finns, it would probably be easier to learn fluent Hindi and Marathi than to swing their hips.

"When our whirlwind of words had died down and I had time to breathe, I felt a tremendous amount of joy. Expressing joy freely is not that typical for Finns or even Indians, but it is still there, waiting to be released. Suddenly, we had a truly Finnish-Indian, or Findian, plan, and instead of a row of OFFs, my schedule now said Takeoff to Bollywood!" explains Helena.

She called a colleague, who appreciated Finnair's slogan "Designed for you", and held all things genuine and home-made in high regard. "With these values in mind, we put together a team consisting of flight attendants, and even one pilot, to work on the plan, which was then put into action on 17 January, 2012 on a flight from Helsinki to Delhi." The video was published on India's Republic Day on 26 January. With the video, Finnair cabin crew sends their greetings to India. You will find it at: www.youtube.com -> Surprise Dance on Finnair Flight to Celebrate India's Republic Day.

I love the sound of aircraft,
the metallic smell of a motorbike,
the glowing embers of a cigarette.

I love the damp grass
of soccer fields
and the winning goals
of ice-hockey games.

Everything about you
melts my heart
to everything that is you
and inside you.

Kati Kaivanto

NO HURRY, NO WORRY, NO CURRY

Several of our flight attendants are bloggers, writing about various work-related issues. Here is an extract from Helena Kaartinen's blog:

A new chapter has been added to my memoir of an accidental tourist. A week spent in Mumbai and the Mahabaleshvar hill station has left a colorful imprint on me. No, I didn't get to meet any Bollywood stars; I received a much better gift. I encountered genuine Indian people and their hospitality. However, sticking to my friend's advice "no hurry, no worry, no curry", which would guarantee my wellbeing in India, proved impossible from the start. I ate more *curry* in one week than I had so far eaten in my entire life. And *hurry* was ever present, since my feet hardly touched the ground as we flew from one place to another.

Soon it was time to fly back to Finland, and I was in for a belly-flop at Mumbai Airport. The check-in clerk looked at me with a face that I hoped expressed merely that he had been partying hard the previous evening, but no. Avoiding my direct gaze, he said in a quiet voice, "There is thick fog in Delhi. We will decide within half an hour, whether or not the flight will be operated today." I soon understood that half an hour is a really long time to be repeating, "Don't worry, be happy!" to yourself. In addition, it was quite hard to look like a carefree travel industry professional, while shifting from one foot to another in time with my new mantra. Finally, we were told that the flight would be operated. Hip, hip hooray! No, not hooray, but hurry. I hurried to the check-in counter, and then to the departure gate, only to face a new setback: the flight would not be operated after all. The apologetic airline personnel were handing back tickets in three different queues. *Worry* had cast its heavy cloak of gloom on those waiting. Apathy had descended – my fellow-travelers looked downhearted and dispirited. All but one man; a man, who apparently assumed that unbridled fury would no doubt give him what he wanted. He raged in every queue, and gave defiant looks to the rest of us, as if challenging us to join in. To the rest of us, however, it was obvious that even if we created a minor demonstration and shouted slogans in unison all around Mumbai, it would not help to clear the fog above Delhi Airport.

I had bought a ticket for the evening flight to ensure that I would make the connection from Delhi to Helsinki in the morning, without any worry or hurry. Now I was full of both, as I ran from one airline counter to another, trying to secure a new ticket for a morning flight. Finally, at the fourth counter, I succeeded, and was given a ticket for a flight that would *maybe* get me to Delhi on time. I settled down with my worry and waited for the morning. I was tired, and probably had "Soon I will burst into tears" written across my face. If I didn't, I should have had, as that's how bad I felt. I was longing for curry. Hurry was waiting on the sidelines, but did nothing to make the hours go faster. I sent a text message to confirm that the flight had left on schedule from Helsinki, and of course it had. I ate a piece of chocolate cake, which was intended as a souvenir, and thought what a short time that first half an hour had been, and how the whole week had gone by so much faster than this one night. I blamed worry and ate the whole cake in retaliation.

When the check-in clerk showed up in the morning, I rushed straight to him. I had reached a point where I could no longer keep quiet about my fears of missing my connecting flight – amateurish, I know, but only human. As I began to share details of my holiday in India, I noticed that the clerk's concentration was no longer at its best. I also noticed the queue that had formed behind me, and decided to head for the departure gate. There was an exaggerated briskness to my walk, as if I hoped for it to rub off on all air traffic in India. Did it have an effect? At least we departed for Delhi on schedule. When I got to my seat, I pulled the blanket up to my ears, deciding to adapt to the role of the world traveler, who is not easily thrown. My mouth was sticky with chocolate cake, and was craving for curry. The Indian man sitting next to me was craving for conversation. "I saw you a week ago, when you came to Mumbai, he said. "Really," I said, and "weirdo", I thought. "I believe we're heading in the same direction," he continued. "I'm going to Riga via Helsinki. I tried to get to Delhi last night, but we circled above the airport, and eventually had to return to Mumbai. I am worried whether we'll make it." I immediately changed my impression about him. Definitely not a weirdo, I thought, but instead, an open and honest person. Someone I could share my worry and hurry with. I would even have shared the curry, but I fell asleep.

We landed on schedule. My new travel companion and I smiled at each other. We had a lot in common: a target, a plan, a shared worry, and we were in a terrible hurry. As we trundled on a bus from the domestic to the international terminal, I felt that we were working towards a common goal, even though we hadn't even introduced ourselves. We sat quietly, occasionally giving each other a little smile, followed by an encouraging nod. I was about to have a hysterical fit of laughter. You know, one of those completely uncontrollable ones caused by a wave of relief, which leaves you unsure whether you're actually laughing or crying. Before I had time to embarrass myself, we arrived at the terminal. Just the last stretch and we would reach our goal. We celebrated with a polite handshake, which, I will admit, was a reasonably modest gesture in relation to the emotions that we had shared.

On the flight from Delhi to Helsinki, I was suddenly aware that there was no hurry, no worry, and no curry. It had all vanished. I surrendered to the emptiness in order to recharge. I thought again about the advice that I had been given. At the end of the day, hurry, worry and curry add wonderful flavor to life. They are available without prescription, but one should not exceed their daily dosage.

CHAPTER 20

THE MOTION PICTURE *FLYING START, DRAGGING FINISH*

SOMETIMES, I CAN'T help but think that life inside a flying tube the size of a house is like a movie. This fictional film begins on a December morning in 2011.

At six am, Leena, a flight attendant and our protagonist, is woken up by loud marching music. The personalized ringtone reveals that the call is coming from Finnair Crew Control. The sleepy woman answers with her first name.

Crew Control: "Hi, it's Kake from Crew Control. I've a flight to Rome for you, and your check-in time is 0705. Landing at 1530. It's a little short notice, but you should make it, right?"

Leena: "Well, good morning to you too. It's my day off, and I've got plans, so I can't do you a favor this time. Sorry." Leena is about to hang up.

Crew Control: "Well, actually, your roster says you're on standby."

Leena: "I most definitely am not! I'm on standby tomorrow, not today. Besides, I've got all these plans."

Crew Control: "Well, how about you have a quick look at your roster?"

Leena drags herself out of bed and to the kitchen, where her roster is attached to door with a refrigerator magnet. She has opened both eyes now, and her expression speaks volumes.

Leena: "Oh crap. I've been looking at the wrong day. Er, how much time did you say I have to get to the airport? I still have to shower and... Oh, crap. I'm coming, but I might be a little late for briefing... but just a couple of minutes… maybe."

Crew Control: "Great. Drive safely. Bye!"

The camera follows Leena, who is now running around like a headless chicken, have a quick shower, put on her makeup and fix her hair while calling her neighbor and all-purpose support person Anni.

Leena: "Good morning, Anni. I'm so sorry to wake you up, but it's an emergency. What do you have planned today? I thought I had the day off, but actually, I'm on standby. Crap. Could you come over and take Emppu and Valtteri to playschool? I don't have time to wait for my parents or sister to get here. I'll be back to pick them up in the afternoon. Could you be a darling?"

Anni (yawning): "Should I come straight away?"

Leena. "If you can. I'll wake up the boys, but I don't have time for much else. You're a treasure."

Leena wakes up the children, kisses them goodbye, puts on her jacket, grabs her handbag, wears her boots, and puts her pumps in a bag. Anni meets her at the door on her way out, and she's off. The sleepy boys are left in the hall, wondering why they don't have the day off after all, as their mother drives away.

When she gets to the Crew Center, Leena notices something different.

Leena: "Oh, crap! Today is *the* day that we wear the new uniform!" She calls Anni, her rock, again.

Leena: "Hi, are you still at my place?"

Anni: "We're just about to leave. What is it?"

Leena: "I'm wearing my old uniform and we should have the new ones on today. Could you get mine from the closet? It's in a transparent bag. Well, many bags, actually. Bring a skirt or trousers, and a top and a jacket. I'm actually in a bit of a hurry. Call me, when you're close to the airport, and I'll come downstairs and pick it up. Thank you so much, I'll make it up to you somehow… I gotta go now. Bye!"

The camera follows Leena explaining to about 100 colleagues, how her new uniform is on the way. She runs into her pre-flight briefing room, and gives an account of the morning's events to the crew. Peetu has his own story to tell.

Peetu: "Hey, not to worry. I forgot my passport and all other papers in the breast pocket of the old jacket. I didn't notice until I tried to get into the parking lot without my ID. Had to call the wife and get her to bring the whole set over. She wasn't very pleased, but brought them anyway. I guess I'm in for a 'performance dialogue' when I get home."

The purser remarks how her children have ear infections again, but this time it's their father's turn to stay home from work to look after them.

The purser starts the briefing. When it's time to go to the aircraft, Anni calls to say she's downstairs. The cameraman can barely keep up, as this ex-sprinter runs down the stairs. Anni gives her the clothes, Leena waves goodbye to her slightly confused-looking children in the backseat, and goes up to the dressing room to get changed. Ouch! Broke a nail. Darn! She remembers that the crew must now wear black pantyhose instead of tan, and rushes to the vending machine to buy some on her way to the aircraft. Of course, the flight is leaving from a remote parking stand, which adds several minutes to the journey. She arrives at the aircraft at the same time as the passenger bus. Leena changes her pantyhose in the rear toilet. An odd thumping and stomping can be heard in the cabin, as her head, elbow, knee, head, elbow… bang against the door and walls. A composed flight attendant walks out of the toilet, now wearing black pantyhose.

It's not exactly postcard weather outside: horizontal sleet. Most of the passengers are not appropriately dressed, and very few have winter jackets on. Two men stand out in their t-shirts, shorts and sandals. These passengers connecting from somewhere where palms grow are cold, of course, and lift their feet as if line dancing, missing only cowboy hats. The line moves very slowly, and stops occasionally. At this point, the camera moves inside the plane. In seat 2D, a man is exercising with his bags: a trolley bag, a laptop case, a couple of tax free bags and a small additional bag. First, he puts both bags and the shopping up in the overhead lockers (pulls up trousers), then the trolley bag down and a newspaper out, the bag up (pulls up trousers), then the laptop case down and work papers out, then the bag up again (pulls up trousers), puts his jacket in the overhead locker (tucks in shirt and pulls up trousers), jacket down again, switches off his cell phone, jacket back up again (pulls up trousers), takes out a tax free bag from under the jacket, takes out cough drops and puts them in the seat pocket, puts the bag up again on top of the jacket (tucks in shirt and pulls up trousers). The line is at a stand-still until the man is finally comfortably seated. He then comments, "They could hurry up and get in already, so that we'd be on schedule. I have an important meeting scheduled at the airport as soon as we get there."

A quick look at the line outside the aircraft: The men in shorts have accelerated their hopping to the tempo of Riverdance, and are no longer smiling as widely. They converse in short sentences.

Back inside, the passengers are intrigued by the new cabin crew uniforms, which they want to touch and ask about – each and every one of them. Some passengers simply stare at the back of the neck of the person in front of them and sigh. Approximately ten people find their seats and sit down fairly quickly, before the next halt, which is caused by a small group of people from Southern Europe seated on rows 8-10, who start swapping seats. None of them actually sit down. A curly-haired woman gets the window seat, but doesn't want it after all, as she has just made an observation: "There's a really big hole on the side and the engine is broken."

The group begins to shout and gesture wildly. The woman's curls bounce from side to side. The flight attendant explains that the hole is not actually a hole, but the door of the hold compartment, which will be closed once all the bags have been loaded. The technical crew is present for a routine check up of the engines, and there is nothing to worry about. The woman doesn't appear to understand or believe anything that the flight attendant says, and wants to leave, because she can sense a "bad vibration". At this point, she hears a "strange noise" as well.

The flight attendant: "All the bags are in, and they're closing the door of the hold. That's what's making noise; it will stop soon."

The woman is not buying the explanation. The purser alerts the baggage handlers that a passenger might want to leave, and if she does, her bag will have to be offloaded. The group is nearly blocking the aisle now, as they all encourage the woman to stay on. Or leave. In any case, they're all behind her, and if she leaves, they will too. The baggage handlers, who should already be at the next aircraft, are now preparing to remove several bags.

A slim, middle-aged, slightly nervous woman is checking and re-checking her boarding card again and again, as she stands in line. The long strap of her bag gets caught on the arm rest several times, and freeing it always takes a little time. Somehow, she manages to slip through the congregation on the aisle. When she gets to row 31, she realizes she's at the wrong row. She had mistaken the gate number for her seat number. She takes her bags along, and once again slips through the "nervous flyer's support group meeting" back to row five. As she goes against traffic, one of her dainty little bags falls down.

Back outside again, where the brave men in sandals are no longer dancing, and not even smiling. They are standing on one foot, "Flamingo-style", warming the toes of one foot against the calf of the other, and blowing on their fingers.

A family enters; a mother carrying a two-year-old girl, three- and five-year-old sons walking down the aisle with their own little backpacks, and last, the father with all the bags. There is a bag for each of the parents, a diaper bag for the youngest child, a toy and book bag, duty free bags, and a bag for snacks. All the bags have to be stowed in the overhead locker *at once*, after which the father proceeds to jump up and down like a jack-in-the-box nine times during boarding, opening bags and digging for items that his wife or the children ask for. Finally, everyone has what they need, and the father starts reading the paper. A flight attendant brings an infant life vest and extension safety belt, and explains their use. Three-year-old Jani-Petteri wants to sit on his mother's lap, while two-year-old Lotta-Juulia insists on getting her own seat.

The mother (to Leena): "Try and use your common sense and understand how much noise there'll be, if I don't humor them. The children will start screaming and crying, and nobody will have a very pleasant flight after that."

Leena: "There is nothing wrong with children who have a strong will, but for safety reasons, the airline's regulations state that an infant under two must be secured with an extension belt and sit on an adult's lap, and a

THE CIRCLE OF DEATH

A tube full of johns and janes
on their way
from America to Asia.
An hour's delay –
smiles and hot towels
what a way to start.

A marathon ahead
New York and aching legs behind.

Beef or bird
flown to you.
– Would you like Moomins or Fazer blue?
– Try the Chanel five!
– The channel or the perfume?

Sit for a moment
before getting up again
– a whisky on the rocks and headphones!
Sand in my eyes, dreaming of bed,
will this ever end?

The last stretch ahead:
heat the omelets and bread,
seal and count the money
if you could.

At the end, a brief moment together
– Thank you for coping so well!

Sirpa Kivilaakso

child over two on their own seat. If they need to cry about it, then so be it."

The Leena explains to Jani-Petteri how the "turbo belt" works, and soon he is happily seated on his own "turbo seat."

A member of the Southern European group informs the purser that the woman will stay onboard. Everyone is relieved. In the mean time, the line for the aircraft has moved at a snail's pace, if it has moved at all. The group decides to swap places one more time. The rest of the world will just have to wait.

Another family is going on holiday that day. They have a teenager, who is allergic to nuts. The parents announce at the door: "Nobody is allowed to eat nuts during this flight, and you need to make an announcement about it, so that everyone will know."

A third family (15DEF), traveling with their baby for the first time, walks in. The flight will be full, so the infant car seat has to be stored somewhere. The baby's pram is already in the hold. The parents are a little lost, but the energetic grandmother starts to organize things. However, she soon discovers that the car seat won't fit in the overhead locker.

Grandmother: "What small overhead lockers you have." (Looks at Leena in disapproval). "Last time I flew, someone had an infant car seat in there."

Leena won't admit to shrinking the overhead lockers, and the grandmother doesn't seem to agree with her explanation that infant car seats come in different sizes.

Grandmother (half audibly, as if to test the audience): "I wonder how that poor child will manage to fall asleep now, being used to her own bed and the pram. It would be so handy, if the baby could sleep in the pram during the flight."

A few young lads (12ABC) have already had a few drinks. The middle-aged men behind them (13ABCD) are also in the mood to party, and so, a bridge across generations has been built. Their volume and the content of their stories require Leena to ask them to keep the noise down. Of course, they can't be expected to know that the woman sitting quietly in 12D is carrying her husband's ashes in her bag and a clenching grief in her heart. She is none too pleased, but can't be bothered to comment. The young man in 12A heads for the toilet, while the aisle is still full of passengers on their way in.

12A: "I'll just squeeze right by here."

At the same time the family in 15DEF decides that now is a good time to change the little one's diaper. After a lot of pushing, squeezing, and waiting to get through the crowd, the couple goes inside the toilet with their baby. Fortunately for the grandmother, the door won't close, so she can stand in the doorway with encouraging comments. She proudly announces her first grandchild's measurements, vaccinations, eating and sleeping habits, and illnesses to the camera.

A few rows down from the allergic teen (21AB) sits a couple, who have a family-sized bag of peanuts with them. The shells spill allover the floor. Leena explains about the allergic teenager. The couple protest, asking on what grounds their right to eat nuts is being restricted. The conversation goes on for a while, but eventually the nuts go in the bag.

Meanwhile, outside: The men in shorts have made it to the stairs and have found caps in their bags to keep their heads warm. One of the caps reads, "The Winner" and the other "I love Bangkok". The Southern Europeans appear to have found a seating order that suits them all, so the line is moving again. Mr. Winner and Mr. I love Bangkok are finally onboard. They notice the new uniforms as ell, but they have a refreshingly new question.

Mr. I love Bangkok: "Is your uniform warm in winter?"

In the rear galley, an elderly nervous flyer is asking for cognac ("doctor's orders, ha ha"), without his wife knowing, of course.

Leena: "Let's just wait until we're airborne, shall we?"

The man walks away.

A nice-looking man arrives in 24F. A moment later, a well-dressed and carefully made-up woman sits down in 24E, but immediately gets up again and comes to the galley.

Mrs. Immaculate: "Are there any free seats? The man next to me has such BO that there's no way I can sit there the whole flight."

Leena: "As far as we know, the flight will be full, but let's wait and see until everyone is onboard. Sometimes a few people don't show up."

The woman goes back to her seat, scrunching her nose. Next the man in 24F wants to get up, and comes to talk to Leena.

Man 24F: "Are there any free seats? The woman next to me has poured a bottle of perfume over herself, which will give me a migraine before we make it to the end of the runway."

Leena: "Really? Let's see what the situation is once everyone is onboard, but as far as I know now, the flight will be full."

The man decides to wait in the galley. Another nice-looking man shows up in 24D. Sits down, but gets up again, and heads straight for the galley.

Handsome man 2: "Are there any free seats? The lady next to me is wearing a lot of perfume."

Leena notices that Handsome man 2 has been visiting the smokers' booth in the terminal more than once, and is now quite "the smoked herring". Leena also sees that Mrs. Immaculate is fanning herself with the safety card.

Leena: "Let's see once everyone is onboard."

She stands between Mr. Sweat and Mr. Cigarette, making small talk about the snowy winter and other light topics of conversation. Both gentlemen decide to go to the toilet, and in the mean time, Mrs. Perfume comes back to the galley.

Mrs. Perfume (Immaculate): "That's an impossible seat. Both of them smell so bad that nobody can sit there. You must have an empty seat. You will try and arrange it, right?"

Leena smiles, and says she understands the predicament... for that entire trio, as everyone around them is getting their share of the symphony of smells – and not appreciating it much, based on their facial expressions.

Leena (looks at the camera, shaking her head): "But what can you do? There's no place to hide."

A woman in a tiger-stripe coat enters with an enormous beehive of hair, and hands a bag of fish roe to Peetu. She wants him to put it in the freezer for her, so that it won't spoil.

Peetu: "I'm sorry, but we don't have a freezer onboard."

Mrs. Tiger stripe: "Oh, don't be silly. I've been served food that's still frozen. You have a freezer. You can put this there, and just bring it back to me when we get there."

Peetu (hands back the roe): "I'm sorry, but we don't have a freezer onboard."

18 basket ball players in uniform enter with bent necks. They're surprisingly agile in sitting down.

The boozers' team on rows 12 and 13 are making wisecracks. The passengers around them are smiling, some openly laughing at the serial crossfire of jokes. Only the widow does not respond; the men assume she doesn't understand Finnish.

One of the last passengers to come in is an assertive man, who shoves his coat at Leena.

Mr. Assertive: "Put that somewhere."

Leena: "What's your seat number, Sir?"

Mr. Assertive: "Look here, I usually travel in business class, but my assistant screwed up my reservation, and that's why I'm in economy class. Besides, that coat cost 2,000 euro, so it can travel in business class even if I don't."

The man continues to his seat. Three connecting passengers don't make the flight, so there are three empty seats, two of them next to each other. This way, Leena can move Mrs. Perfume to an aisle seat, with an empty seat in the middle of that row. There's a man sitting in the window seat with a beige jacket. He nods shyly, and then continues to look out of the window. After all, what could be more interesting than the weather outside? The man is too shy to say anything, even though the woman's perfume irritates him as well. Easier to breathe, looking at the rain and the scenery.

The fourth flight attendant, Maria-Sofia, checks for any more infants onboard. She hears little snippets of conversation here and there. "Look, there's like an old flight attendant!" "That other one is a bit fatter." "Last time we flew, two flight attendants had like really long legs. Almost too long." Right. Only two infants.

Somehow all the passengers and their belongings are finally in their appropriate place, and the flight attendants begin securing the cabin. A few bags are sticking out of the lockers, so a relocation of baggage has to be conducted before the aircraft is ready to go.

The purser begins announcing, "Welcome onboard this Finnair flight to Rome…"

There's restlessness in the cabin, and heads are turning. The passengers are going to Malaga, but the aircraft and crew to Rome. The Southern Europeans begin an animated conversation. The camera moves outside. Which bags have been loaded onboard? Rome. The bus has brought the passengers to the wrong aircraft!

The camera returns to the forward galley. Several phone calls are made to various places. The decision is made in two minutes. It is quicker to keep the passengers onboard, and only move the luggage. The aircraft and crew will then go to Malaga. Leena send a message to her parents, saying that her work day will be at least four hours longer than planned, so could they go and pick up the boys from daycare.

There seems to be an army of employees outside. Fairly soon, the aircraft is ready for departure to its new destination. The crew carries out the safety demonstration and check the cabin for takeoff.

Peetu: "Could you please switch off your cell phone?"

Passenger 18E: "It's in flight mode."

Peetu: "Yes, but the power has to be switched off during takeoff."

Passenger 18E: "Hey, it's in flight mode."

Peetu: "I understand, but you need to switch it off for takeoff."

Passenger 18E: "Hello, it's in flight mode! Do you know what that is?"

Peetu. "Yes, I know what flight mode is, and I have it on my cell phone too, but the phone still needs to be switched off for takeoff and landing."

Passenger 18E: "Jeez, that's just so old-fashioned."

Peetu: "Yes, I agree, but so far, those are the rules. You need to switch off every device that has any kind of battery during takeoff and landing. Even if it's a balloon with a light on it."

The aircraft is waiting for takeoff clearance at the end of the runway. On the window seat 23A, a man suddenly remembers that he has forgotten to switch off his cell phone, which is in his jacket pocket in the overhead locker. Stepping on other people's toes, he scrambles up, and starts looking for his jacket under a stack of bags and coats. The cabin crew has given the "cabin ok for takeoff" notification to the cockpit, which have, in turn, given it o the air traffic control. A quick call to the cockpit. "Not ok after all." The man finds his jacket, but accidentally pulls out a handbag, which is unzipped, and all its contents fall out. Peetu is quickly on the scene, closes the overhead locker, asks the man to sit down, and returns to his crew seat. The air traffic control is asking for a reason for the delay, because there is a long line of aircraft waiting to take off. A new "ok" notification to the cockpit, the engines roar, and the aircraft finally takes off. Pens, keys and lipsticks are rolling on the floor towards the rear, but passengers manage to pick them up and send them back to the owner. Apparently she manages to get everything back, because nothing is reported missing.

The safety belt sign is switched off. The toilets immediately have long queues outside them. At this point, the camera shows a 360-degree view of the interior of a toilet, or, as one should say, "Ladies lounge". After all, that's clearly what it is, with its makeup table and scented soap. The makeup mirror is wall-length, which gives the space an airy feel,

and the room has been lit as one, harmonious whole. The relaxing seat is only a quarter of a step away. A changing area has been designated for infants. The middle of the room leaves some space for dancing. The colors are light, reflecting Scandinavian simplicity, with an aura of uncluttered Feng Shui. The slanted ceiling gives an intimate, cottage-like impression. There is calming music in the background (if you whistle).

Leena is hunting for her apron.

Leena: "Oh, no! I have my old uniform apron! Never mind, then I just won't wear one.

She then changes her boots into pumps.

Leena. "Oh, you gotta be kidding me!"

Maria-Sofia: "What's the big deal? You just won't wear an apron, it's ok."

Leena is already wearing one shoe; the other is on the floor, next to her. Both are for the left foot. Luckily, the purser has an extra apron and an extra pair of shoes (just two sizes too big). What to do, but to go with what you're given.

The bearded man from 30D comes to ask for two cognacs right after takeoff.

Bearded man: "It's the wife's birthday, so we're celebrating a little."

The man gets his drinks and returns to his seat. The basket ball players' legs criss-cross the aisle.

Maria-Sofia: "I think we'll have to carry the trolleys, when we get to them."

The meals have been heated and packed in the trolleys, the coffee and tea brewed, The drink trolley "set up", and the aisle cleared of obstructions (bags, legs, feet, pillows, blankets, hanging safety belts, children's toys). Leena pulls her drink trolley up to the curtain, followed by the meal trolley and two other flight attendants. The allergic boy has spotted another aircraft from the window, and his father gets up to look out as well. In order to keep his balance, he stretches his other leg out on the aisle. Leena trips on it with her spacious shoes and flies right into a passengers lap, hitting a few people on the head as she flails about. Not exactly a controlled landing – 0 points for style. The other shoe flies off her foot, and catches a passenger on the cheek. Since the aircraft is still climbing, the drink trolley slides down the aisle, and hits Maria-Sofia's ankles. Bull's eye! Coffee and tea spills out of the pots, on to the arms of people in the aisle seats, and on Peetu's hands. He gives out all the napkins from on top of the trolley, and goes to get some more from the rear galley. No casualties, but a few minor injuries here and there. The man is genuinely surprised at how his leg could trip up anyone. Leena apologizes for all the pain and suffering she's caused. The caravan continues its journey towards the business class curtain, with one flight attendant limping, another shuffling along with large shoes, and the last with stinging hands.

The service can finally begin. A few rows are completed with fairly ordinary requests and pleasantries. A short man, who's apparently fallen into a barrel of beer, is seated on the fourth row.

Mr. Hops: "It's ridiculous that there's so little leg room, and the seat-back is barely at an angle, when I put it all the way down.

Leena: "I'm sorry. It's true that modern aircraft don't really have a lot of extra space. Just asking what you'd like to drink with your breakfast?"

Mr. Hops. "Listen – I'm an old army buddy of your CEO's. Give us a couple of beers to make up for this crush, or I'll make this into a big thing."

Leena wonders how the CEO knows so many people, because there are army and golf buddies, school mates, and college friends of his practically on every flight. All in all, company appointments that are discussed in the media seem to generate a great influx of army buddies on flights… Maybe that could be used as a marketing gimmick in the off-season?

The familiar tiger-stripe woman (23E) with diamond-studded glasses would like some champagne.

Mrs. Tiger stripe: "It's just something that you do. And it's my style."

The family in 18CDEF would like the infant's food heated.

Mother: "Just 30 seconds on maximum."

Leena: "I can heat it, but we don't have a microwave oven. I need to heat it in hot water, and that takes a little longer."

Mother: "What do you mean you don't have a microwave?"

Leena: "Aircraft usually don't. It'll take about 10minutes to heat the food. I'll bring it back to your seat when it's done."

Mother: "But Lotta-Juulia is hungry now."

Leena: "Do you have something else with you that you could give her?"

Mother: "No."

Leena: "Well, if I just warm it a little for five minutes? Would that be ok?"

Mother (tight-lipped): "Yes, I suppose it's fine."

The snack bag contains candy.

Leena follows the meal trolley with drinks.

Passenger: "Give me vodka."

Leena: "With or without ice?"

Passenger: "Sure."

Leena: "Would you like anything else?"

Passenger: "The sprite."

Leena: "In the same or different glass?"

Passenger: "The same, of course, I asked for vodka with sprite!"

Leena: "Five euros, please.

The man pays with a 50-euro note. Leena asks the woman sitting next to him (who turns out to be his wife) nearly all of the same questions, and gets nearly all of the same answers. She wants to pay with a 50-euro note too. There's not a lot of change onboard.

Leena: "Er... Would you have a smaller note, or perhaps a card you could pay with?"

The wife: "No."

The man: "Fine! I'll pay this time then."

He hands Leena a 20.

The man (to his wife): "You can pay me back when we get there."

Leena wonders if they have separate rooms booked.

The limping caravan continues towards the rear, but the journey is somewhat jerky, as the trolleys go back and forth in order to let people pass on their way to the toilet or back to their seats. The flight attendants apologetically ask passengers to mind their belongings and knees. The latter is difficult for the basket ball team, but they do their best. In spite of precautions, the meal trolley bangs into a player's knee, and three meal trays tip over. Peetu scrapes the sauce off the carpet, and takes the trays to the galley, bringing back Lotta-Juulia's food at the same time. The girl has already let out a high-pitched reminder. The mother offers a poopy diaper in return.

Peetu: "We're handing out meals... Could you put the diaper in the plastic bag we gave you at the beginning of the flight, and take it to the waste bin in the toilet later on?

Mr. 29D: "I'll have a beer, four cognacs, and an orange juice. The wife's birthday, you know."

Leena congratulates the wife. She lifts her eyebrows and thanks her, smiling. On row 31, Leena asks what another mother is about to drink.

The mother is about to open her mouth, but is interrupted.

The father: "Two brewskies."

Leena asks the mother again, but before she can answer, the man interrupts.

The father: "Yeah, two brewskies and two red wines as well."

Leena thinks that he is ordering for them both, and hands them each a beer, a wine, napkins and cups. The man moves them to his own tray table, and pokes his wife in the side.

"Well, tell her what you want!"

Before the mother can answer, her teenage daughter places her own order. Finally, the mother manages to ask for a wine. When it turns out that you have to pay for alcohol, the wines are returned. The mother now has nothing to drink.

The father (not looking that happy): "So, what's free then?"

Leena: "Juice, water and soft drinks."

The man: "Well, give her a juice then."

Leena is trying to look the woman in the eye, but she is staring at the seatback in front of her.

After the meal service, the woman from 29E joins the queue for the toilet. Maria-Sofia wishes her happy birthday as well.

The Birthday girl: "Yeah, right! Firstly, my birthday isn't until April, and he doesn't remember it anyway. Secondly, I don't even drink hard liquor. He's just using it as an excuse to get drunk."

She slips into the toilet.

18F puts his seatback down. 19F glares at him, but doesn't say anything. Instead, he grinds his teeth, and you can imagine his blood boiling. He moves to the next level, by firmly grabbing 18F's seatback, and giving it a good shake. 18F doesn't take a hint, so 19F shakes the seatback again, this time with more force. 18F turns around.

18F: "Jjfhno nfwei fcof? Kbdyrue sdkgjh fkeshf kjfe. Kdjherhoeihtsbritght."

19F: "Sorry."

This doesn't end here, thinks 19F, and decides that what goes around, comes around, and lowers his seatback with one jerk, which knocks over 20F's wine and water glasses. He, in turn, decides to teach19F a lesson by giving his seatback a good shake.

19F: "What's wrong with you? Don't touch my seat!"

Soon there's a full-blown war. The wives decide to participate actively as well, with high-pitched shrieks.

18F: "Ybbadfi dhf fuyevs."

Apparently he is saying that he wants to sleep, but seems wide awake.

On the other side of the aisle, Lotta-Juulia is frightened by the noise, and starts crying, with Jani-Petteri soon joining in. The five-year-old is concentrating on his PSP game, and the father is reading a paper. The mother tries to calm her children, and complains about the "small Gaulish village."

The Mother: "Grown men!"

20F goes to clean himself up in the toilet, and 19F comes to the galley for a victory cognac. When 20F comes out, 19F offers to buy him one as well. They shake hands, and the matter is settled.

The children finally calm down. Jani-Petteri is swinging his legs while drawing, and accidentally kicks the seatback in front of him. The camera moves to the woman sitting in front of him, who is our old acquaintance Mrs. Tiger stripe. We see how her face tightens, and she eventually turns 180 degrees in order to share her views on manners.

Mrs. Tiger stripe: "Now, you beautiful boy, don't kick my seatback. I have the right to a peaceful journey." She continues, this time to the mother: "Very cute children, but as a mother, you really should teach them some manners. Rule number one: don't kick my seatback." Lotta-Juulia is clearly scared of this "my hair is my crown" woman. Her mouth begins to twitch, and soon both children are howling again. The father continues reading the paper, and the big brother's focus is on the PSP game. The mother doesn't have time to say anything in defense, as Mrs. Tiger stripe has plenty more to say.

Mrs. Tiger stripe: "Ah, there they go again! When do you think they'll stop? They're ruining the whole flight! Tell them that I insist that they stop."

She smiles at the children, but the smile doesn't reach her eyes. She turns around and sits down again. The children calm down soon after that. Two champagnes later, Mrs. Tiger stripe falls asleep with her mouth open, and snores loudly.

Mrs. 19E and 20E are still at it. The men return, having settled their differences, and the couples discover that they are staying at the same hotel. They soon begin planning excursions together.

32D comes to buy a couple of more "brewskies".

Leena: "Anything for your wife and daughter?"

32D: "Just give them some juice."

Two Asian passengers come to the rear galley to exercise, while the cabin crew has their breakfast. Soon, 29D is back to ask for some more birthday cognac.

Leena: "You're a considerate man, making your wife's birthday into such a big thing. I can only imagine what great surprises you must have in store for her, once you get there. I wonder if your wife would consider you to be overly romantic, if you took her some champagne."

The man: "Oh. Would that be a good idea then?"

Leena: "Of course. You can't go wrong with champagne."

The man: "Fine, I'll buy her one then. I don't really care for it myself, since it has those bubbles and all, and tastes quite bitter… but I'll take one for her."

Romeo goes back to his seat. The wife is pleasantly surprised, and winks at the flight attendants.

Mrs. Tiger stripe, who has lived half her life in Texas, has woken up from her nap, and is coming to powder her nose. She starts talking to the crew, asking questions and answering them herself. Her hair bounces and jewelry jingles as she gesticulates. The cabin crew listens and nods – there's really no chance of getting a word in edgewise.

Mrs. Tiger stripe: "Do you actually understand at all, what I'm saying?"

The cabin crew: "Yes, yes, do carry on."

All three nod, trying to finish their breakfast at the same time.

Mrs. Tiger stripe: "Just wondering, since I'm talking to myself here. You Finns are so shy, all of you. You should participate a little. Have you not been taught any small talk? You're following so far behind. You wouldn't get very far in the U.S. that way. You need to know how to talk. Even if you just say: 'Interesting.' That would be enough, really. You can study conversational skills at university in the U.S. At least in our university in Dallas. You should come over – even if it's just for a short course or something.

Fortunately for the crew, a toilet is now vacant, and Mrs. Tiger stripe goes in. Jani-Petteri has found his way to the galley as well, and begins to fiddle with the megaphone and fire extinguisher, which are attached to the wall. The mother finds it very amusing.

The mother: "Our future fireman…"

The cabin crew asks that he not touch the emergency equipment. The mother thinks that they are rude, and have no consideration for a child's natural curiosity.

The mother: "I can tell you don't have children of your own."

The line for the toilet gets longer and longer, and the older representatives of the boozers' team are on the move. The men buy some drinks while waiting for their turn. They tell the crew how on their last rip, their luggage had failed to come, and it had rained the whole week. The men had worn the same clothes the entire time, as it was raining so hard it rinsed them off nicely. Their suitcases had appeared at the door the day before their return flight. Apparently, the suitcases had been left behind at the airport, and been outdoors the whole week, because all the clothes inside were wet and had grown moldy. The men threw everything away. This time, they were only carrying passports and money. After all, what else does a man really need on holiday?

The woman in 12C opens the overhead locker, which the man in11C had closed, and a half-liter "song book" in a duty-free bag falls out. Fortunately, the man has bent to tie his shoelaces, and the bottle only hits his back. He lets out an understated "Ouch", and raises his eyebrows slightly. (This role will require someone, who can express 10 phrases and at least five different emotions silently with his eyebrows).

The crew is selling, and while Peetu is closing the deal with a passenger, Maria-Sofia chats with an elderly woman about her travel plans. The woman says that she is on her way to her son's holiday home. She hasn't traveled very much, and this is her first trip on her own.

The little old lady: "I'm a little nervous, but you're all very nice to a little old lady."

Maria-Sofia is a little surprised, and touched by how the woman clutches her hands.

Maria-Sofia: "Thank you, but we've not done much for you…"

The little old lady: "When I told the new deaconess from my parish that I was going on this trip, she told me that if you walk in looking assertive and proud, and appear richer than you are, you'll get better service onboard. 'I can't do that, I thought,' and luckily, there's been no need to."

The sales are completed, and the flight attendants take the trolley back to the galley. The wife on row 31 is embarrassed by her husband starting to slur, so she closes her eyes and pretends to sleep.

13A, who is traveling on business, hears passengers a few rows ahead of him ordering drinks, so he puts up his hand too.

The business traveler: "Could I have a diet coke, please."

Leena takes the order, but back in the galley, she notices that diet coke is finished, and she needs to get some from the forward galley. On her way, she takes a few more orders, and stops to answer people's questions. How much time left? What's the local time? Where do the buses for down town leave? Or is it better to take the train? What if we take a taxi, how much would that cost? What's the distance from hotel X to tourist attraction Y? Is it within walking distance? What's that city on the left?

Since getting his diet coke seems to take a long time, the business traveler asks for it again, this time from Peetu, who is collecting trash in the cabin. Peetu goes back to the galley, and starts looking for diet coke, but as he is now alone there, he also needs to serve customers showing up at the back and asking for drinks.

The business traveler is getting increasingly impatient, and decides to try a third flight attendant. Maria-Sofia takes his order, but as she returns to the galley, she sees the ashen-faced widow come towards her, and then collapse on the floor. Maria-Sofia manages to catch her and cushion her fall a little. She lifts her legs up, loosens her tight clothing, and checks if the widow is breathing. Peetu comes to help. In a little while, the widow comes to, and is able to sit up. The crew gives her some juice. The purser comes to check on her, but as the patient is now doing better, she returns to serve business class passengers.

Maria-Sofia (to the purser): "Could you take a diet coke to 14A?"

The purser gets the diet coke from the forward galley, and takes it to the passenger, who, of course, hasn't asked for one, but is thirsty, so he only says "thank you" and smiles.

The widow insists she is feeling better, and returns to her seat.

Maria-Sofia goes to the forward galley to get a medical incident report form, but notices on the way that 13A is still missing his diet coke, so she goes to get one.

Leena finally returns from the forward galley with a mountain of supplies for the rear, and hands out a diet coke to 13A. When she gets to the galley, Peetu takes a diet coke from her, and takes it to 13A. Mr. Business traveler is now sitting with three diet cokes in front of him, and thinks that the flight attendants are being nasty. When he seems upset, they explain what happened.

Mr. Business traveler (directly to the camera): "Yeah, right. They just forgot about my order."

Leena is restocking the bars for the return flight. She is crouching by the trolley, and holding a full case of soft drinks in her lap, in order to free her hands. The portion milk in her apron pocket is squashed and breaks. Leena begins wiping the apron and skirt. A little girl comes to ask for a Fanta. Peetu is crouching to take one out, when the aircraft hits some clear air turbulence or "a bump" in colloquial terms. Peetu hits his forehead on the counter, and as he gets up, he hits the top of his head on the door of a catering box that has opened, and with the next bump, he hits the back of his head against the wall. As he clutches his head, he knocks over a juice carton, and its contents are spilled over Leena, who has fallen on the floor. Now her new clothes are covered in milk and juice, and her back and behind hurt. There is a small gash and a red bump on Peetu's forehead, which begins to turn blue on the return flight. There are soft drink cans here and there. The girl has fallen down too, but is not hurt. She takes her Fanta and goes back to her seat. The can has been shaken, so as she opens it, its contents sprays all over her. Nothing new there, then. The flight attendants knock on the toilet doors, and ask if the people inside are ok.

After the turbulence, Leena and Maria-Sofia decide to do "a water round", with cups in one hand, and a bottle of water in the other. The aisle has become an obstacle course, with shoes, blankets and pillows all over. The passenger in 28D shifts in his sleep, so that Maria-Sofia, walking backwards, trips on the passenger, and the water bottle falls in his lap. He wakes up wet and – refreshed. As she stumbles, Maria-Sofia manages to knock another passenger on the head, and, as she falls down, she falls on the arm of a woman taking something out of her bag, so that the woman's arm is caught between the armrest and the flight attendant. Her arm is hurt, and needs to be treated with cold towels. There is a rush of apologies all around. The good news is that as a result, all the passengers are now awake for landing. The exhausted Asian passengers are opening their eyes, and Mr. Winner and Mr. I love Bangkok crawl out from beneath their blankets.

Just before the landing gear comes out, and as the plane shakes in the strong side wind, Jani-Petteri has to pee. The mother cannot understand why the flight attendants won't let him go to the toilet. He's just given up diapers, and can't hold it in for a very long time.

The mother (in an accusing tone): "He'll pee his pants then."

Leena explains that wetting his pants is the lesser evil than him getting injured in the toilet.

The mother: "I would look after him. He wouldn't get hurt."

After landing, the parents are angry, because the boy's pants are wet now, and he doesn't have a change of clothes in their hand luggage. After the family is gone, the flight attendants find two poopy diapers in the seat pocket, next to the empty plastic bag.

The handsome Mr. Sweat takes his souvenir bag from the overhead locker. It's filled with various kinds of cheeses wrapped in paper. Five hours in room temperature has done its duty, and the aromas are stronger.

Passenger 22C: "Where can I ask for compensation for my white jacket? The dirty wheels of someone's trolley bag have ruined it! And besides," (he sniffs the jacket); "It smells like sweaty feet! Who's paying for this?"

The passengers leave the aircraft in a much more orderly fashion than they came in.

Mrs. Tiger stripe: "I need to get off this plane! I'm in a hurry!"

The purser: "And where are you going, Madam?"

Mrs. Tiger stripe: "To a better future!"

The purser: "Oh, really? I didn't know they still had flights there."

The man standing behind Mrs. Tiger stripe winks and asks, "And on which airline?"

One more passenger slips into the toilet. The queue halts for a while, just as Mr. Shy is leaving. Maria-Sofia asks him how his flight was.

Mr. Shy: "Oh, very nice, thank you."

He smiles and blushes a little, but he doesn't really have the courage to look her in the eyes. A cloud of perfume seems to follow him.

A young man in 28E is looking for his cell phone. The man is not aware that it fell out of his pocket during landing, slid to the floor and all the way to row 24, where it has now been buried under trash. There is no way of noticing it. The mother helps Lotta-Juulia and Jani-Petteri with their clothes. The father takes all the bags, and steps on the cell phone (yes, it's broken now). The young man is still looking for the phone, and assumes it has been stolen.

Young man in 28E: "A cell phone can't just vanish! Someone's taken it while I was sleeping! This is going to cost your company; I'll make sure of that!"

(Soundtrack for this scene: a symphonic version of Queens' Bohemian Rhapsody).

As Maria-Sofia is saying goodbye to the customers, a passenger hands her a paper bag.

Passenger: "My daughter's been sick in this."

Maria-Sofia has to hold the bag as she says goodbye to the rest of the passengers. Lovely. The cleaners come on board, and the crew tells them about seat covers that need changing. The cleaners discover that the girl had been sick already once before. That time, the mother had apparently put the bag on the floor, and afterwards, somebody had stepped on it. There is an empty vodka bottle in the seat pocket at 31E. In addition to the floor, also the seat pockets at row 21 are full of peanut shells.

During the turnaround, Leena switches her phone on and notices she has a message. She assumes it's from Anni, saying something along the lines of, "The children are at playschool and everything is ok." Instead, it's a message from the playschool: "Emppu fell from the swing. He has a concussion. He's at the hospital under observation, and your parents are on their way. Don't worry."

Leena calls Finland.

Leena: "How bad was it? I can't get there for another six hours. Emppu's father is away. Thank you for letting me know, and thank you for calling my parents. Are they there yet? Can I speak to Emppu?"

The playschool teacher: "He's asleep now. Your parents will be here soon."

The aircraft is ready for boarding, and for the entry of another mini-community. In spite of the nice people onboard, for Leena, the flight home seems very long.

CHAPTER 21

INTO THE FUTURE

TODAY, PASSENGER JETS carry people from one place to another at a speed that we could only dream of in the past. We've come a long way since the Wright brothers' combustion-engine aircraft. The work of the cabin crew has become more hectic, and there is not as much time for interaction with passengers as there used to be in the past.

Departure 2093 was published in honor of Finnair's 85th birthday. It offers interesting views on air travel in the future. The future might offer passenger cruises in space, and aircraft that are faster than the speed of sound.

In the 1960s animated series The Jetsons, the characters moved from one place to another with vehicles that were a hybrid of cars and light aircraft. It is possible that one day, air space might indeed have to make up for congested traffic on the ground.

In the future, supersonic aircraft might be used for intercontinental flights. These aircraft would be shot from long catapults. The jet and rocket engines would lift the aircraft up to a very high altitude, and the vessel's wings and rudders would fold away, transforming it into a space shuttle for the rest of the journey. On the other hand, passengers that are not in a hurry could opt for a Zeppelin-like airship, which would glide at a speed of 300 kilometers per hour towards its destination, or perhaps merely cruise above interesting places. With an increase in automation, the role of the cabin crew will change as well. Hopefully, it will mean more time for passengers.

THE MULTINATIONAL FUTURE

Airlines are experiencing turbulent times. Multinational airlines already exist, traditional airlines employ increasingly multicultural staff, and joint ventures are formed. Who knows what the future has in store for Finnair cabin crew? One thing is certain at least: no matter what kind of aircraft we fly in, we will still be there for passengers. My favorite story is the story of a young woman, who got the job of her dreams, working for a well-known, international airline. That airline could never go bankrupt – and yet, one day, it did. She still loves her job, and still flies, but for another airline...

The creators of this book all share a love of flying. Joy and wistfulness go hand in hand, as we look back on the past and our memories on these blue-and-white wings. We don't know what the future holds, but when a door closes, a window opens, and a new opportunity may present itself. Come what may, the spirit of togetherness among Finnair crew will always live on.

We thank you, dear readers, for this journey from the doorstep to the far edge of the world and back. We look forward to welcoming you onboard again soon!

I FLY AS A BIRD

I fly as a bird
in my metallic body
above clouds of cotton.
I whisper your name
  in the dark of the night.
How beautiful you are.
A memory of the past,
almost forgotten.
I whisper your name
in the pale light of dawn.
How beautiful you are.
Is it the heavens that
  brought us together?
So beautiful, so warm.
I whisper your name
in the blue light of dusk.
From one continent
  to another
I carry you inside
  my metallic body.
I whisper your name.
It echoes back
  in everything that I am.

Riitta Kiiveri

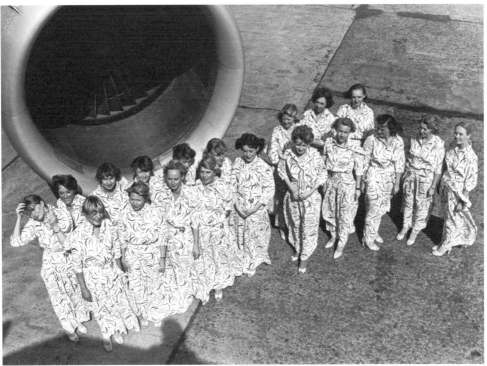

THANK YOU

I WOULD LIKE to warmly thank everyone, who had a part in creating this book. Thank you to those numerous flight attendants, who shared their stories with us. We received valuable photographs and newspaper articles from contributors' personal archives. Our book required long hours of voluntary work, and people offered their help with only altruistic motives. The writers' rewards will be donated to the Finnish Central Association for Mental Health's "Princess" school campaign, which provides support for children and young people.

Finnair gave us access to its photo gallery, and supported us with an open mind. These stories would not exist without our blue-and-white wings.

The association of retired flight attendants, Evergreens ry, notified its members about our project, and many of them contacted us, invited us to their homes and spoke with us for hours.

Cartoonist Ami Niemelä and illustrator Kati Kaivanto are members of our work community, as are poets Sirpa Kivilaakso, Kati Kaivanto and Riitta Kiiveri. Our customer Lauri Saari wrote a lovely poem for our cabin crew in Bulgarian air space on the way back from Cairo.

Thank you to our publisher Thor-Fredric Karlsson (Atar Kustannus). Juhana Mikkanen designed the lovely layout.

Our team was photographed at Niko Fagerström's studio. Johanna "Pinksu" Marjomaa was responsible for the makeup, and flight attendant and hair stylist Pauliina Honkavaara for the hair.

The management of data and sources would have been impossible without Tony Pokkinen's "StoryBank" database, with which we processed over 1,000 text and photo files.

Our test readers Anne Luomala-Eriksson and Tero Kokkonen gave us valuable information about the reception of our stories from the viewpoint of the general public.

Editor Tarja Lipponen worked patiently with our stories. Journalist Varpu Helpinen read the text once more, and gave some additional advice.

Purser and translator Nana Arjopalo translated our book into English.

Thank you for your stories and photos: Maaret Ahokas, Jutta Alberdi, Katri Alén-Kettunen, Ulla Alkio, Anne Andersson, Maija Anttila, Suvi Anttonen, Nana Arjopalo, Minna Arola, Anna Aukia, Päivi Aurekoski, Ursula Backman, Maija-Liisa Bennett, Gerhard Berger, Joakim Boije Af Gennäs, Heidi Borg, Semi Broström, Susanna Bäckman, Laura Böstman, Satu Eckhardt, Helena Eklöv, Marjo Elo, Kristina Etelävuori, Minna Fagerström, Niko Fagerström, Teija Fagerström, Pigga Filenius, Sasa Färling, Gina Gröndahl, Bobby Gull, Irina Hahl, Satu Hakala, Tytti Hakala, Teea Hakanpää, Sanna Hanttu, Jatta Harkonsalo, Leena Harkonsalo, Anne Heikkinen, Kauko Helavuo / helavuok@saunalahti.fi, Kati Henriksson, Hanna-Lena Herronen, Hele Hintikka, Mari Hollmen, Miia Holopainen, Pauliina Honkavaara, Annika Häggman, Mira Hämäläinen-Iho, Taina Ihalainen, Viveka Inkiläinen, Sanna Iso-Antila, Nina Isomaa-Friman, Theresa Isännäinen, Heidi Jaari, Marissa Jalasvirta, Jussi Jouppi, Jukka Järvi, Helena Kaartinen, Riitta Kaila, Tuula Karppinen, Carita Kauppinen, Kirsimarja Kavasto, Sari Kemiläinen, Kaisa Ketolainen, Sirpa Kivilaakso, Katja Knichter, Emma Koivuluoma, Marko Kokkala, Petri Kokko, Susanna Kokko, Annika Korpela, Anne Kotakorva-Stanley, Elina Kovanen, Johanna Kuure, Mirja Kynsijärvi, Tiina Kåla, Susanna Kämäräinen, Paula Kääpä, Pirjo Lahti, Meri Laihonen, Hannu Laine, Marjo Laitala, Ranja Lammi, Heli Lankinen, Tania Laporcherie, Riitta Laru, Sari Latvalahti, Aaro Laukkonen, Kai Laurmaa, Susann Lehtimäki, Lena Lehtonen, Taina Lehtonen, Petra Lempiäinen, Tuula Lerkki, Mari Leskinen, Varpu Lilius, Marjo-Riitta "Markka" Lindholm, Riitta-Liisa Linnapuomi-Jaari, Satu Lonka, Kimmo Lucander, Timo Luoto, Monica Löflund, Tina Lönnqvist, Mia Maikola, Kaisa-Sofia Malinen, Tarja Mattsson, Mona Mervasto, Merja Metsola, Elisabeth Meurman, Annastiina Molin, Kaija-Kristiina Muilu, Jarmo Mänttäri, Helena Määttänen, Birgitta Nevalainen, Minna Niemi-Gerlander, Ulla Niemi-Pynttäri, Ulla-Kristiina Nousiainen, Vera Nyqvist-Hertzberg, Johan Nyström, Tiina Nyström, Anna Ojaniemi, Sari Orava, Maija Outinen, Petteri Paasikunnas, Mari Pakola, Anna Palho, Antti Pekari, Annukka Penttilä-Eriksson, Minna Penttilä, Tom Penttinen, Laila Pietikäinen, Petri Pihlajamaa, Satu Piipanoja, Nora Pirttijärvi, Eija Pitkänen, Tiina Puranen, Pertti Purkunen, Ville Päiväniemi, Liisa Pöyry, Hannu Raikkala, Pirita Rainisalo, Anne Raiskila, Heli Rajanen, Elina Rantala, Tuula Rapp, Outi Rautalahti, Jutta Rinne, Irmeli Ristiluoma, Raimo Romppainen, Annette Romunen, Tuuli Rosti, Ingela Rotkirch,

Anita Rousselot, Anna Ruskokivi-Kanerva, Suvi Saarela, Lauri Saari, Tiina Saarikangas, Minna Saarniaho, Sannaliina Saine, Marika Sampio-Utriainen, Nina Sapman, Charlotta Savander, Mirjam Seilo, Annika Sharp, Minna Stoilov, Mia Sundström, Teija Suojanen, Arja Suominen, Antti Suopajärvi, Nora Sylvander, Jaana Sylvin, Elina Syvähuoko, Sanna Särkikangas, Ulla Tapola, Ullamaija Teutari, Tiina Tikanoja, Susanna Timonen, Ari Toivonen, Hanna Toivonen, Arja Tuomarila, Tomi Turkkila, Heidi Ukonaho, Eerika Utter, Meri Utter, Anna Vahala, Gunilla Wahlberg, Päivi Vaininen, Katri Vainio, Réa Vainio, Henrietta Valli, Elina Vanhala, Laura Varja, Susan Weckström, Riikka Vennervirta-Zisis, Kirsi Vestenius, Arja-Leena Viertola, Katja Viianen, Anne Vilkman, Emmy Westerback, Tiina Wilkman, Karin Viloma, Sanna Winberg, Sari Vinnari, Lotta Winter, Anne Virta, Hannele Wollin, Anna Wollsten, Riitta Vuorelma, Timo Väliviita, Anni Väyrynen, Eeva Ylismaa, Mia Ypyä, Crew Service Desk.

Flight attendants on a picnic in Helsinki Kaivopuisto park in summer 2012. The "Siipien Havinaa" ("whispering wings") event brought together over 80 flight attendants. The furthest visitors flew in from Canada to meet their ex-colleagues.

WE THANK OUR COOPERATIVE
PARTNERS AND SPONSORS FOR THEIR GENEROSITY AND SUPPORT

ALEKSANTERIN
TEATTERI

Osku Heiskanen & Jarkko Valtee
www.showhat.fi

Ellen Jokikunnas

Marco Bjurström

Arja Tuomarila & Kai Lind

Kiki Rautio

Photo by: Tomi Salmivuori

www.sisdeli.fi

www.artfilmsproduction.com

www.familyinc.fi

www.futureimagebank.com

www.miraculos.fi

www.socks.fi

dpn®

DESIGN PAULA NUMMELA

www.dpn.fi

www.luottokunta.fi

www.fiblon.fi

FINNAIR CATERING

Mann's Street

www.mannsstreet.com

COVER PHOTOS

Photography: *Juhana Mikkanen* www.juhanamikkanen.com
Lighting: *Lari Heikkilä*
Studio: ImageBank/*Niko Fagerström* & *Juha Reunanen*
Makeup: *Johanna "Pinksu" Marjomaa* www.pinksu.com
Hair: *Pauliina Honkavaara* www.hiushuonelennokas.fi
Hair products: Paul Mitchell www.miraculos.fi
Props: Penny Lane/*Ritva Wächter* ja Aleksi 13

PUBLISHER

ATAR PUBLISHING

THOR-FREDRIC KARLSSON

It is truly fantastic to find people with such big hearts who are willing to work so hard in order to help others. I congratulate Finnair for having such wonderful employees! It is worthwhile to hold on to them and to take good care of them. I trust this crew and continue to have the courage to fly high in the future too.

THE FLIGHT ATTENDANT ON THE COVER

FINNAIR FLIGHT ATTENDANT

TIINA NURMI

I began my career as a flight attendant at Finnair in 2007. I was very pleased and honored for having been given the opportunity to be on the cover of this book. The photo shoot itself, together with the book committee, makeup artist, hair stylist and photographer, was an unforgettable event full of laughter. The charity we are supporting is very important to me personally, as I am a mental health and substance abuse worker by my other profession. The proceeds of this book are directed to those who truly need help, and I am very proud to be able to participate in this charity.

THE GODPARENTS OF THE BOOK

MEMBER OF THE PARLIAMENT OF FINLAND

JAANA PELKONEN

It is heartbreaking that more and more Finnish adolescents are in danger of being socially excluded or are otherwise mentally unwell. This should not be the case.

The importance of community and caring can never be emphasized too much.

It is important that with a book like Airborne: Tales from a Thousand and One Flights, we can help young people with a positive twinkle in our eyes, and hopefully make mental illness less frightening and easier to understand by everyone.

Photo by: Janne Torikka Photography

A 7 YEAR OLD

JANI-PETTERI

COMEDY CHARACTER IN THE FINNISH TELEVISION SHOW "PUTOUS" (SEASON 2011-2012)

Hi, I'm Jani-Petteri, a seven-year-old first grader and a godparent of the book Airborne: Tales from a Thousand and One Flights. Yes! The Finnish Central Association for Mental Health's "Princess" school campaign aims at diminishing inequality and offering a perspective on bullying at school, which stems from a fear of the unfamiliar. Being different is beautiful. I would like to recommend this book to one loud-mouthed imbecile, whose name I shall not mention: Tero Högfors.

OUR NOMINATED CHARITY

THE PROFITS FROM the book are donated to the Finnish Central Association for Mental Health, to be used in the prevention of mental health issues among children and adolescents. The association is currently running the Princess campaign in schools, arranging viewings of the Finnish film Princess, followed by discussions led by mental health professionals and peer trainers. The peer trainers consist of people of all ages, who have suffered from mental health problems in the past, and now

PRINSESSA-koulukampanja

give talks about illness and recovery. In these events, young people are offered the opportunity to speak about difficult issues, and many have found a peer group or the means to seek professional help this way.

Every school classroom in Finland is estimated to include one to two persons who suffer, or whose parents suffer, from psychiatric problems. According to the National Institute for Health and Welfare, 60 percent of young people whose parents have mental health or substance abuse problems, will have psychiatric problems before the age of 26.

Finnair cabin crew chose this charity cause by majority vote.

Mielenterveyden
keskusliitto

LIST OF SOURCES

Escolme-Schmidt, Libbie. *Glamour in the Skies: The Golden Age of the Air Stewardess.* The History Press, 2009.

Haglund, Christer et al.*Departure 2093: viisi visiota lentomatkailusta.* Toim. Maria Mroue. Finnair Oyj, 2008.

Huttunen, Anja-Brita. *Ammattina lentoemäntä.* Toim. Erik Rissanen. WSOY, 1984.

Hytönen, Yki. *Viisi vuosikymmentä lennossa: Finnairin lentoemäntien ja stuerttien työn historia 1947–1997.* Edita, 1997.

McLaughlin, Helen E. *Footsteps in the Sky: An Informal Review of U.S. Airlines Inflight Service 1920s to the Present.* State of the Art, Ltd., 1994.

Raikkala, Hannu. *English influence of the speech of Finnish Airline Cabin Attendants.* Thesis. Helsinki School of Economics, 1975.

INTERVIEWEES

Ulla Tapola (Fligt attendant 1953–1955 and 1959)

Réa Vainio (Flight attendant 1956–1958 and 1987–1992)

Riitta-Liisa Linnapuomi-Jaari (Flight attendant 1956–1970)

Helena Määttänen (Flight attendant 1959–1971)

Maija-Liisa Bennett (Flight attendant 1963–1975)

Marjo-Riitta Lindholm (Flight attendant 1965–2001)

Hannu Raikkala (Flight attendant 1972–2006)

Outi Rautalahti (Flight attendant 1979–)